Motorcycle State of Mind

Motorcycle State of Mind

Michael Stewart

CONTENTS

PART ONE: PRE-RIDE   1

1   Gotta Go   3
2   Before Motorcycle, After Motorcycle   10
3   The Itch Grows   15
4   All Of Us Explorers   19
5   Disclosures   23

PART TWO: THE RIDE   27

6   The Send-Off   28
7   Road Vomit   33
8   Ride The Ferry   40
9   Fountains   42
10   The Road   53
11   Gas Stop   58
12   Little Big Horn   64
13   Magic Carpet   68
14   A Bridge   79
15   Squirrels and Impermanence   84
16   Astoria   86
17   Honest Pie   90

| 18 | Coffee Stops 102
| 19 | Balance, Brakes, and Beliefs 108
| 20 | Be Flexible or Stay Put! 119
| 21 | Rolling Stones, Rolling Wheels 127
| 22 | Driving Blind 140

| PART THREE: GOTTA RETURN 144

| 23 | Home Isn't The Finish Line 145
| 24 | Disconnected, But In Gear 158
| 25 | The Last Ride 163
| 26 | Read The Signs 167
| 27 | Home Base 173
| 28 | Lopsided or Balanced? 176
| 29 | Saved by Cycle 178
| 30 | Immunity 183
| 31 | So What? 186
| 32 | The Final Revolvement 188

| ADDENDIX: Break In Procedure 189

BOOKS BY THE AUTHOR 191

PART ONE: PRE-RIDE

He who has a motorcycle can bear almost anything.
—— Friedrich Nietzsche (Paraphrased)

Preface

The Scraping Pegs books encourage readers to reflect on the motorcycle experience, apart from riding skills and the mechanics of the machines.

However, the Appendix provides some assistance regarding break-in procedures.

1

Gotta Go

The great myth is that you need a dream bike, an exotic locale, loads of money, time, full gear, and a fill-in-the-blank to achieve the perfect ride. You don't—but it's easy to believe if you're lazy, timid, jacked up on adrenaline, narcissistic, recovering, or simply living your life. Changing perceptions can be a son of a bitch.

I was stuck in the mud—mentally uncertain, emotionally stalled—when my Guzzi riding friend Marta kick-started things. "Juggling is always going on in the background. Mike, it's time to step up and challenge your beliefs ... to tune your Motorcycle State of Mind."

It'd been three years since my last road trip—three years since the stag Horace the Horrible sent me flying into asphalt on Highway 20. The itch hadn't gone away. I'd just been nervous about scratching it.

"Oh, sweet mother of motorcycle mercy," I muttered. *What d'you want from me, Marta? Why must you complicate everything? Just let the wheels roll.*

But then Conrad added, "Yup. Time to pack your bag, Mikey."

"A road trip, you say?" The proposition had merit. "Tell me more."

* * *

Once, the mere thought of a motorcycle road trip had me imagining I was Ernst Shackleton.

On December 5, 1914, a three-masted barquentine christened Endurance departed South Georgia, an island southeast of the Falkland Islands, bound for Antarctica. "For king and country," Sir Ernest told his wife, Emily. "Gotta go." He presented the concept one evening over dinner. It had to do with planting a flag at the South Pole.

"A higher calling, Ernie? Really?"

Ernest didn't attempt to justify "the explorer state of mind" or "when the sea and ice call, you gotta go." Pointless. Some have the yearning; to others, exploration and riding the waves are daft notions.

"At least go somewhere nice ... We could all go. Take the train and the kids. Pack a lunch."

Ernest felt guilty, but the sea called. It wasn't the first time he'd fled to the wild blue yonder. Emily wept, thinking *Gotta Go* meant cold-hearted, callous abandonment. "What is your problem, Ernie? I'm not enough?"

Ernest didn't attempt an explanation. The fact of the matter is ... He could have added, "It's not you," but his attempt would have been futile. Probably made matters worse. The ocean calmed Ernest and his mind was at ease, knowing his beloved was devoted to their children and domestic duties.

"You see how it all works out?" Marta would say. "Some explore. Others tend the home fires."

Conrad's take? "If everyone went, it'd be a shit show. A pig's breakfast, like riding on a badly balanced wheel."

South Captain Shackleton sailed to the Weddell Sea, where *Endurance* became stuck like a dirt bike bogged down in wet clayish mud. Pack ice trapped *Endurance* and slowly crushed it.

Imagine your bike stalled on a freight train crossing. Along comes the 12:45 bound for Shit Creek. You climb off and jump to safety, but your helmet got crushed—you can't put it down, wait for another biker to spot your distress signal, and feel obligated to rescue you. How about the time you were you stuck with a broken chain and no cell service?

Riders might not haul sleds across ice fields to whaling stations to be rescued, but many have pushed and pulled heavy bikes through shit to rescue themselves.

"What do you have to say for yourself, Ernie?" Emily demanded when her husband returned three years later. "Now that the kids have grown without a father?" She didn't mention Jack Clarkson from down the lane who wanted to ride her like a whaling ship.

Three years and still miffed, Ernest thought. How can that be? He shrugged. It was an early case of *The Worst Trips Make the Best Stories*, but the paradox was lost on Emily. It wasn't long before Ernest's itch returned. He said, "Johnny Rowett wants to do a Beaufort Sea run … on a converted Norwegian sealer."

"For the love of God, Ernie, you haven't had enough penguins?"

The Beaufort is in the penguin-less Canadian Arctic, but Mr. Shackleton didn't spell it out. He twitched. Why bother? Pointless.

But he was not blind to the fact—Emily's logic made some sense. Stay home where it's cozy in the warm, loving embrace of family. There's no getting around it—as with riding the waves, placing yourself in harm's way on two wheels disrespects the survival instinct. There is no obligation to climb on. No one has to go.

* * *

"Gotta Go is a stake in the ground," Marta continued over coffee at Tony's Deli.

"A wind therapy," SQUID Dolores added.

"The opposite of baseball's safe at home," Earl said.

"Can't rely on ball players for discoveries," Den said. "They all want to stay on base."

Explorers feel yearnings they must appease. The risk of tragedy is ignored. Funds are diverted. They abandon loved ones. Mr. Shackleton spent many miserable months marooned on Antarctic ice. Still, he climbed back on. It's a head scratcher to many.

"Has to do with his mindset," Marta will tell you.

"And the itch," Conrad would add. "Always the itch."

Later, at home, when I mentioned "road trip," Dori, my wife, said, "Go ahead. Have fun, Mike." If she was seeking to be nice, Dori would have said "Michael" and spun my world upside down, leaving me hogtied by sweet logic and weighted down by guilt. "Almost got yourself killed three years ago. Didn't learn a thing, did you, Mike?"

Objections to *Gotta Go* cannot be put to rest by attempting to explain the magic of two-wheel that called me or the urgencies that dwell in the explorer's mind. Over the years, one comes to understand—it's pointless. My friends have a label for those unable to comprehend: "NimRods."

How much easier it would be if the itch was explainable, but attempts to enlighten only lead to bitterness and never-ending squabbles. Perhaps a bike forced off the road. "Who's the NimRod now, biker-idiot?" cagers swear.

"Enjoy playing with your toy."

"Thanks," I said, responding to Dori's sarcasm. "I certainly will."

With that I was locked in. Gotta go.

* * *

Had motorbikes been available in Shackleton's time, an excursion around County Kildare would have sufficed. Emily would serve tea, while Cecily and Raymond helped Daddy polish his forks. Today's explorers have it easy. Gotta go? Check your tire pressure, grab your credit card and climb on.

Sailing ships were a rudimentary forerunner of the motorcycle road trip—the wind bore down, demanding engagement. Hoist the mainsail! Lower the boom! Stow the jib! Heave to. Man overboard! That sort of thing. Yet the art of sailing pales compared to riding. Why? Water, water, everywhere.

The sound of synthetic rubber on asphalt, or the feel of a tire digging into dirt, trumps a hull pushing against water. It's essential to brain balance; for some, it's a mother's loving embrace.

After sailing to Antarctica, Sir Ernest proposed to walk across the continent and back, a distance of 1,800 miles. Traveling on water alone was not sufficient to scratch his itch. His crew pleaded, "We've seen the snow, ice, and penguins. Why not turn and head home, Captain? Stop off at one of those tropical isles like Ferdinand. Explore their beauties."

"Gotta go," Ernest mumbled about his overland expedition. Sailing wasn't enough.

Bonkers, his crew thought. How do we get through to this guy?

"NimRods," the captain swore.

Motorcycles resolved the shortcomings early explorers faced. Where ships trapped men in cramped quarters and tedious weather delays, bikes offer instant escape. If Magellan had a two-stroke, he might've blown past all that colonial mess and ridden solo into the sunset.

Adventure isn't in the distance—it's in the motion. And motorcycles provide that in a way wind and sails never could.

Ferdinand led five ships—Before Motorcycle, going solo was not possible. Imagine two-hundred-and-thirty-seven riders. When the *Santa Maria de Victoria* reached the Philippine archipelago, Magellan and his gang charged ashore, eager to violate and subjugate. Like a pack of bikes going into a curve full throttle, someone would end up in the ditch.

What if Ferdinand had been born hundreds of years later? The magic of a 1930 Ossa two-stroke could have satisfied his *Gotta Go* urge. He'd climb on and ride south from Sabrosa. Therapeutic powers would blow Biker Ferdie's pious, overzealous demons away. In the heart of Africa, Ferdie would smile and say, "No need to convert. Let us scrape pegs together, friends." Early African Motorcycle Dreamers would smile and fantasize about owning Ossa motorcycles one of these days.

Had Africans owned motorcycles, they could have evaded the slave trade.

* * *

Early explorers relied on belief. Riders also look beyond the horizon. Gotta Go is not just about rebellion or freedom—but belief in the journey.

We don't ride because it makes good sense. We ride because it makes life better and so our inner Shackleton and Magellan urge *Gotta Go*.

Like explorers, riders move on—there is more out there. It's why some leave their jobs, partner, home to go for months or years. Or why others pack light, ride hard, and return to wait for their next journey.

Belief is the fuel that keeps explorers going.

Marta says a motorcycle would have changed upgraded Magellan's mindset. He'd be like the guy who used to paint on PBS. "Go out on a limb—that's where the fruit is."

My motorcycle possesses a bit of Endurance, the need to explore, and the willingness to accept consequences. It loves to paint pictures and show me works of art. Keep moving toward the horizon where the black line meets the sky. That's where the fruit is.

The more I thought about Sir Ernest, the more the road called to me as sea lanes beckoned Ernie. "Gotta go."

Dori continued to roll her eyes. Early on we rode two-up, but togetherness changes over time.

It's too bad they stopped mandatory premarital blood tests. Testing ensured forever compatibility at the cellular and plasma levels and helped avoid defective infants. It was the same idea as manufacturers' oil specification and warranty warnings included in owner's manuals. The right formulation prevents overheating, increases fuel economy, and prevents engine wear. Today, there are no boundaries, so blood tests are taboo.

"Don't dismiss doing your own Motorcycle Compatibility test," Marta advises. "You don't need to go to a lab, just ride … two-up. Do multiple trips, at least one in shitty weather. Ask yourself, Is three a crowd? It sure was for me." Guzzi ended Marta's brief first marriage.

While enjoying coffee and cinnamon rolls at Tony's Deli, Earl posed this question: "What if your kid turned out to be imperfect thanks to no premarital blood tests? Imperfect Kid uses out-of-spec oil and wrecks your engine? Then your partner whoop-de-do's because she'd always resented your bike?"

Despite being outlaws, we agreed, some regulations make a lot of sense.

* * *

At home, I worked on my trip preparations.

In my early days, packing demanded ingenuity. How do I lash all this stuff onto my It'll Do Bike without a rack? Now that I have the appropriate gear, I rarely camp, and I've learned that with good balance, life on the road requires little. There's no telling how far you can go with a few provisions.

Sir Ernest needed investors and sponsors to purchase a ship, buy provisions, and hire a crew. Motorcycles, being affordable, are a game changer.

"Call you Ishmael," Marta said when I told her I had a departure date.

"Who?"

"Ishmael," she explained.

Like Shackleton, the sea called to Ishmael. He found himself on the whaling ship Pequod under Captain Ahab. "I will have revenge!" Ahab swore. "Gotta get that fucker!" The giant white sperm whale, *Moby Dick*, had chomped off Ahab's leg at the knee on Pequod's preceding voyage. *Moby Dick* and *Horace the Horrible* (the vile kamikaze stag who took my GT down three years earlier) were cut from the same cloth. There are killers in the water and on the land. Explorers have always been targets.

"Call you Ishmael" was Marta's way of reminding me: Go, but be aware. Captain Ahab, Moby Dick, pack ice, kamikaze beasts, and other perils are real.

"Sometimes it's smart to keep a toe on home base," I said.

But I couldn't.

I gotta go to scrape my therapy.

I had the itch.

2

Before Motorcycle, After Motorcycle

Marta, an engineer and history buff, whittles time down to two distinct eras: Before Motorcycle (BM) and After Motorcycle (AM). "Motorcycles were the turning point. First the Big Bang then, in 1885, came the evolution of 'it's round and it rolls.'" A vague attempt, but how do you explain the MAGIC and the JOY of two wheels?

Marta's division of time demonstrates her out-of-the-box thinking and causes NimRods to roll their eyes. Doesn't matter—there's no denying the invention of the motorbike was a great wheelie forward. Gotta go? After Motorcycle there was a practical solution.

"Folks like Hannibal had the inclination, but not the means. I think of him as the grandfather of outlaw riders," Marta says. "He rode hard, but the poor man was doomed to fail."

The Carthaginian general chose elephants for their low-end torque. "Perfect for climbing the Alps," he told his commanders. His crew packed thirty-seven of them—their version of adventure bikes. Enormous, high-maintenance, and, like SQUID Dolores, prone to panic near cliffs. Picture it as a thirty-seven-bike group ride with no sweeper, tons of actual shit, no GPS, and one guy in leather sandals claiming he knows the way. It was the original large group ride — guys losing sandals, elephants squatting, refusing to move, morale tanking. No intercoms or cafés. Just trumpeting and Hannibal yelling, "Gotta go."

Taking an army over the Alps on elephants was gutsy. No spares, no maps, no heated gear—just a war vibe. Hannibal rode the way some riders tackle road trips. Try doing the trip on a rusty dual-sport with bald tires, **a** worn clutch, and no spare gas container.

On the far side of the mountains, the boys raped, pillaged, and enslaved until Hannibal's campaign failed. Elephants don't lean and there's not enough wind therapy to cure the barbarian state of mind.

Not enough wind. No pegs to scrape. No countersteering. Hannibal swallowed poison in the Bithynian village of Libyssa. The townsfolk cursed "elephant-idiot" in a Before Motorcycle language.

In Hannibal's time, the feelings that ignited explorers were repressed. "For my Lord," was the pat answer, "I must go." Muffled by societal norms and plagued by a lack of technological sophistication, Hannibal could only express himself through rape and pillaging. A progressive, compassionate society would have extended understanding and forgiveness, along with a safe drug supply of mind numbing drugs. Instead, they labeled our grandfather a barbarian and exiled him.

Hannibal was like a diabetic before insulin. A schizophrenic before fluphenazine. An explorer Before Motorcycle. Tour guides agree—it's the kind of journey riders romanticize until the saddle sores set in.

Today, Mr. Barca would be a respected leader of the pack. He'd own several bikes.

He'd have his own YouTube channel.

He'd volunteer at the Pachyderm Wildlife Sanctuary.

We kicked this around at Tony's Deli—soon to be just "Tony's," with a new bistro-style menu and fake plants.

There was agreement on the bottom line.

"It was a shit show Before Motorcycle."

* * *

The grandmother of bikers? Marta suggests it's the exquisite Lady Godiva. Her tyrannical, I-know-what's-best-for-serfdom husband gave her the itch.

"Gotta go," Godiva vowed.

Her husband, claiming divine right as ruler of Coventry, England, had levied another oppressive tax. Pompous despot! Godiva didn't dare utter the words, but she flipped her spouse the first reported use of the biker salute. A bit of a joker, her overlord retorted, "I'll roll the tax back if my lady rides through the streets stark naked."

Ride, Lady Godiva thought. What a splendid idea!

She mounted her steed, waist-length hair her only shield. Bloody brilliant! Godiva rode, giving her jackass-in-charge spouse the middle finger—'gotta go, asshole.'

The Lord of Coventry lowered the tax boom anyway—"So, you're a political scientist and a macroeconomics expert now, are you, Godiva? Rider-idiot!" He prohibited his lady from climbing on and directed his knights to apprehend the pervert Peeping Tom.

"There's something about a woman in the saddle," Tom stated in his defense.

"Very much so," the knights admitted before they executed their prisoner. "But we're not in charge." Feeling awful, they went for a gallop once the job was done.

"Not only did Lady Godiva ride, she defied," Marta says. "Proving you don't have to lie down under the man's tread."

"But the person with the most displacement generally wins," Conrad stated.

"Had it been After Motorcycle, Godiva could have rounded up the gang."

"Kicked the lord's ass."

"Or just rode away."
"Think she'd wear gear?"
"Be a shame," Earl said.

* * *

Den, the reader in our group, said, "It was the era of darkness. It was the age of despair. It was the time Before Motorcycle."

"States of mind were gloomy," we all agreed.

"No ability to twist the throttle ... ride it off."

"Escape bleakness."

"Imagine if Charles Dickens had been able to ride," Den went on. "What his books would be like."

"David Copperfield would have pulled wheelies. Way more interesting."

In Dickens's time, the search for balance was a dead-end street ending in loneliness, scurvy, or a similar debilitating burden. Some early adopters took up jogging. Patellofemoral Pain Syndrome (runner's knee) goes back to the Garden of Eden. Jogging eventually piles stress fractures on top of loneliness. So, many of our forefathers switched to sailing. "Seasickness is better than runner's knee and fractures," crews agreed. Research shows it was the rum and exploitation talking.

Today's compromised joggers switch to golf and drink scotch in the clubhouse after cursing missed putts. Mark Twain said that golf is "a good walk spoiled." The sportswriter Jim Murray said, "Golf is not a game, it's bondage."

Motorcycling has its great book—no one has written *Zen and the Art of Golf*. Explorers ride the Road to Joy. Golfers sit on carts waiting for Arnold to find his shanked drive.

Marta promotes multitasking. "Motorcycling improves lesser activities." JOY requires periods of not riding. So continue to golf, jog, walk the dog...

Writing saved Mr. Dickens from golf. However, in 1842, Charles came down with the itch. "Gotta go, England," he declared as the steamship Britannia departed Liverpool bound for the New World. He compared his cabin to a giraffe forced into a flowerpot. Reading Mr. Dickens's report, it's easy to imagine him on a motorbike road trip complaining about handlebar vibrations, the Ass Problem, and potholes while praising the glory of exploration.

"The guy sure looked like a biker," Den said.

Had Mr. Dickens lived a century later, he would have authored the best-selling motorcycle book of all time: Charles would write, 'There's no need to squat cross-legged on a mountaintop. Buddha rides in the electrics because he understands motorcycles are a perfect environment.

"Imagine Charles Dickens's Spirit of Motorcycling Future pointing from the grave," Den suggested.

"Spirit!" Scrooge cried, tightly clutching at his robe. "Hear me! I am not the man I was. I understand trail braking and have known the MAGIC in the machines." His vision ends with Tiny Tim receiving a new bike and an approved helmet from Ebenezer. "Ride, lad. Don't turn into a joyless miser like me. Don't be a Dreamer. Climb on! Explore! That's the ticket."

Kickstands up!

3

The Itch Grows

The itch can throb like alcohol rubbed into a bee sting—Gotta go. Gotta go. Gotta go.

When we gonna go? Get the hell outta Dodge?

Pound! Pound! Pound!

Damn this static life! Hit the road, Jack!

We were back at Tony's, chewing on philosophy and cinnamon rolls.

"Never been stung by a bee," Marta said. "Pull over. Let them fly away. They gotta go too. Make honey."

"Wasps are a different story."

"Like hornets. They don't have a driving force. No honey queen to tend to."

"We all need a raison d'être."

"At least the French," Conrad said.

"Don't be reckless with gotta go," Marta warned. "Scratch too hard and you bleed. Some overdo it. Tip the scales and lose balance. Their motorcycle state of mind not engaged."

"Like when I switched from plain M&M's to the peanut ones?"

"Or porterhouse rather than sirloin?"

"Stepped up to brand-name synthetic oil?"

Marta rolled her eyes.

Of course we understood, but getting Marta's goat amuses.

There are many in-the-moment urges. They lead to fat, addiction, porn, imprisonment, and other assorted miseries or time wasters. If you're six, you spend your spare time collecting sports cards or doll outfits. Later it's video games before moving on to tomfoolery. We must take stock and then the time to fashion our well-being. For those at Tony's, the conclusion—the best place to do that is on-motorcycle.

"Dial in your state of mind and while you're at it, pound a stake in the ground," Marta suggested while wagging her finger at me. "Don't just climb on and ride away."

My eyes glazed over. My friend often goes too far. *What's wrong with just riding, Marta? Twist the throttle, scrape your pegs, clear your head. Park your bike and then repeat.*

My itch was growing, and I had a short trip planned, but I didn't think of it as a soul-searching quest. I'm a simple man. No need to plant a flag on the summit of Mount Everest or win the Isle of Man TT. I have a modest bank account and a few good friends and have learned to ride without guilt. All I need is a little time in the saddle to reset. I'm not crucial to the operation of things, so when I hit the road, there's no need to worry about life falling apart. It takes some miles for that notion to sink in, because we are so very important in our own minds.

Believe me, life will cope. It couldn't care less. Just ride.

Marta waited for more, so I played along. "Are you suggesting I should have an objective, more than making it to my stop for the night, like exploring Mars on an electric bike? That sort of thing? Or maybe patenting a cure for the Ass Problem?"

"Not something preposterous. Don't set yourself up to fail."

"For example?"

"Come back a better rider."

"Or maybe a plan to ride on every continent," Earl suggested.

"You'll bankroll me?"

"Mindset is within your control. Not constrained by time or money," Marta said.

"Restore old bikes," Conrad suggested. "On the cheap."

"Use your road trip to elevate your state of mind," Marta continued. "That's your mission." She paused. "Here's the thing. Each day make at least one revolvement."

"Revolvement?"

"It's a word. Look it up."

"Revolve, like the turn of a wheel?"

"Or, turn of the mind."

"A wheel breakthrough," Manny said.

Marta smiled. "A change of state." She paused. "So, what'll it be, Mike?"

I shrugged.

"You must have something."

I gave it some thought. "To see if I can still push off. Test my toe. Determine if the itch is real or just a phantom impulse."

"Do not doubt the itch," Conrad said.

SQUID Dolores suggested, "May be continue … all the way to the Arctic Circle. YouTube it. It's the last unexplored motorcycle road."

"I'd subscribe," Den said.

"I'll need a crew of volunteer flunkies," I said. "With deep pockets."

"So?" Marta asked.

I looked her in the eye. "Marta, I'm ready to count my revolvements."

I think I had the Gotta Go itch way back in Grade Four. I remember writing a report on Louis Jolliet. Unlike the other kids who picked Amelia Earhart or The Great One, I picked Jolliet because he was an explorer, the first European to map the Mississippi River.

Jolliet and a priest and five other explorers were sent to see if the river flowed west to the Pacific. It didn't. But the team made the best of things and followed to the Arkansas before turning around and returning home. A thousand miles in a birchbark canoe. Three months. Six portages. Four snake sightings.

"Jolliet!" I announced. "He didn't have a grand purpose. He just went to see. No dream. No calendar. Just an urge to go."

"Sounds like an influencer of his era," SQUID Dolores said.

"Just a guy in a canoe," I said.

"With vision," Marta said.

I once met a rider who had a vision—she trained for a solo cross-country charity ride like it was the Olympics. She dedicated herself to a routine that included yoga and strength training, along with the development of her social media profile and detailed route plans. "You've got to track results," she told me.

I remember drinking a smoothie with her. I thought about how poor my grip strength was, thanks to my accident, and wondered if I should start doing pullups. Usain Bolt stretches before sprints.

Later I did a lunge, twisted my hip, and had to ice it for three days.

Tony brought a tray of fresh cinnamon roll pieces. "On the house."

"Don't leave with nothing," Marta said.

"Nothing?" I waved a cinnamon piece.

"No conviction, no plan to boost yourself. Get over your trauma."

I took a bite. "Just a ride." Columbus didn't have a clear objective. His pitch to the queen was: "India, Your Majesty. On the cheap." We know what happened. He just wanted to go, and that led him to where he ended up. "But I may come back a changed man. Could happen."

Marta picked up the smallest cinnamon piece. She looked pleased.

4

All Of Us Explorers

Ernest Shackleton was not an affluent man. He received little assistance from governments or businessmen. Gold? Beaver fur? Slaves? No? Then why go? You want to go to the South Pole because it's there and you have an itch? How about picking up a load of tea on the way back? Or opium?

Establishment bodies like the Royal Geographical Society weren't much better. Fortunately, there were dreamers in the Before Motorcycle era. Folks captivated by the idea of discovering the world but unwilling to commit to an expedition. Thanks to inheritance and exploitation, aristocrats had deep pockets. Before Motorcycle, Dreamers liked the idea of having a hill, boat, or glacier named after them, as long as someone else did the exploring. Ernest found financial backing.

Today, cavalcades of Motorcycle Dreamers squander money on packaged all-inclusive vacations to world wonders and lesser, on-the-beaten-path tourist destinations. They don't stop to think, 'I could've stayed put and supported someone's two-wheel exploration.'

For five large, we'll name a piss stop after you, buster. But Motorcycle Dreamers opt to use their money to purchase souvenirs and then drift away, back to their humdrum lives.

Politicians of all stripes are even worse. They're dismissive and needy. Take. Take. Take. Despite two-wheel efficiencies, there's not a single motorcycle tax break, touring grant, or even a respectful nod. The people-in-charge print money to buy votes, but none of it's thrown motorcycling's way. Inclusivity hasn't crossed the two-wheel curtain. "It's fuckin' discrimination at it's worst!" Conrad says.

I agree. Politics is essentially a coalition of the well-meaning but perpetually unbalanced.

"All government bodies should be forced to ride," Marta says. "And don't come back until you have a Motorcycle State of Mind."

That's not what happens, but we have an out. Our ace in the hole?

Climb on. Scrape pegs. Then hold up the biker salute as you pass the legislators.

Give society's laws and norms the finger.

Elections are as necessary as oil changes. Like oil, governments get dirty—no matter the brand, shit piles up. The Tony's gang has adopted the diaper change approach to voting. Clear the shit and repeat.

It'd be nice to have a fairy godmother, but the reality is money does not fall from the sky to finance wind therapy. Instead, riders must use old-fashioned self-reliance. Live within our means. Budget for necessities. Make allowances for extras such as speeding tickets and medical emergencies. When times are good, we add a farkle or two. When times are tough, the Tony's gang says:

As Manny puts it, 'If you ain't got the do-re-mi, don't ride!'

With motorcycles, it's possible to have more fun with less costly machines and gear. Marta's well-used Moto Guzzi is a good example.

Sleeping in a tent instead of shelling out for a motel bed is Bull of the Woods Manny's approach. He likes to quote Bob Marley, "Some people are so poor, all they have is money."

I have a touch of somniphobia—fear of falling asleep outdoors—fueled by ophiophobia, the fear of snakes slithering into my sleeping bag while my riding buddies snore in neighboring tents. So, no camping on this trip. But I'd be reasonable. Early Americana accommodation, the down-and-dirty network of motels, would suffice. A short tune-up trip wouldn't bankrupt me. I wouldn't be trying to reach India.

The one thing I couldn't afford was excuses; complacency can seep in like sweat on a helmet liner. Before you know it, I could find myself towing a tent trailer.

"On your trip, don't spend like politicians," Marta warned. "You can't raise the tax rate to balance your budget or artificially jack up the money supply. Investing in yourself doesn't mean breaking the bank."

Marta was right: you need money to ride, but you can't buy a well-balanced state of mind.

"We could apply for a research grant to study your recovery, Mike. Or wind therapy in general," SQUID Dolores suggested: use the money to fund your trip."

"We'll all tag along."

"As research assistants."

Professional engineers add credibility, so it was worth considering having Marta make a submission.

"Get real," Conrad said. "Pointless."

"Like Why do chimpanzees throw their feces? One million, five hundred ninety-two thousand taxpayer dollars." As usual, Marta was loaded with facts. "Do horses prefer bananas to carrots? Two million, one hundred eighty-six thousand dollars. Do ovulating lap dancers get higher tips? Many twenty-dollar bills. Does toast fall on the buttered side? One hundred twenty-seven thousand, six hundred forty-three dollars."

Tony interrupted. "Enough!" As a small businessperson, he has a low threshold for government waste.

Marta winked.

The gang understands—there is a price to be paid for giving society's laws and norms the finger. If we applied for five hundred bucks, our application would be rejected, stamped:

DENIED! Biker-Idiots Need Not Apply.

Unlike space explorers, lap dancers, and social causes, bikers are not valued.

I shrugged. "I'll dig into my pockets. It'll be fine."

"I'll pack a lunch or two," Tony offered. "If you wear a new Tony's tee shirt."

"Throw in a cinnamon roll?"

Tony nodded. "Everyone gets a tee shirt with my new logo."

"Two for this guy," Marta said. "He'll need a change for his trip."

Shirts, packed lunches, cinnamon roll. I was off to one hell of a start. Ernest Shackleton never had it so good.

5

Disclosures

"Please attend to the garbage, Mike, before you leave."
Mixing trash with Anticipation JOY is repulsive, but while on garbage duty, I had a brainwave: Riding is disposing of mental trash!

Thank you, Dori, for giving me a trip slogan, something I can offer Marta as a revolvement. My Anticipation JOY skyrocketed. "Any more garbage to take out?" I couldn't wait to get underway and dump my rubbish.

"No, but could you..." *Remodel the kitchen. Pull the weeds. Bulk up the bank account.*

"Busy," I replied. "Must update my GPS."

Let's take care of a few other chores before I hit the road.

My Motorcycle

Are you curious about my machine? It has a brand, model, and specifications—my motorcycle is not non-binary or motorcycle queer. Like all machines and riders, it dropped onto the sales floor with design intent.

"Motorcycle style and culture are a spectrum," SQUID Dolores says.

True. People tour on 150cc scooters. Cruisers become café racers. Trikes have adventures. Still, bikes are pigeonholed. Humans like to label things.

To avoid typecasting, my bike's brand, model, and style will remain in the closet.

This book is about the MAGIC in the machine and tuning up. There will be no dyno readings, turning radius specs, spring rates, paint codes, or other shop manual topics. My motorcycle, Neuro, will travel incognito.

Everyone knows Superman is Clark Kent. He is in love with Lois Lane and is suspicious of Batman and Robin's relationship. But who is Neuro (short for Neuromodulation Machine)? Neuro is steadfast, impish, lightly farkled, and one hell of a ride. It's hard not to gloat, but I will restrain myself.

Modulate me, Neuro! I tingle every time I see my buddy—he can send out a wink and light up the sky like the Bat Signal.

Before Motorcycle explorers never exclaimed, "Modulate me, Santa Maria!" Shackleton never glanced back over his shoulder at Endurance and thought, What a beautiful hull you have! Constantly, bikers are drawn to the allure of steel and then swell with pride of ownership.

Know that Neuro never makes a false step. My bike will forge ahead and gain the advantage when called upon. But I need not hurry; Neuro will be patient with me. We get along remarkably well.

Marta gave me this advice: Remember, you're not going to the track. Balance is not a race.

Before going down hard, Mikey Boy had a reputation for getting carried away. Once spanked, your perspective changes.

My Route

Wondering where I'm headed? The Stans? Mongolia? Alaska? No, I'll be touring a speck of the world. Close to home base, but far enough to be called out. I must return in time to take the garbage out.

It's a trip we've all made. No support vehicles. No fancy camera gear. No visas, spare tubes, or gas containers. No need to say, "Sayonara, old life! I'm riding away to start fresh."

I wasn't. *I shall return!*

Riding can be extraordinary, even close to home. Every trip holds the chance of curveballs—that's what keeps it honest. You don't need a YouTube channel to validate your ride. Same roads, new perspective. "It's okay to repeat," Marta says. "If your mind's tuned in."

"Boring is part of life," Cam said. "Accept it, Marta. No matter where I've traveled, it's weighed on me. All those miles bearing down and grinding it out, struggling to make it through mind-numbingly boring surroundings."

We've all been put to sleep by Mother Nature's dodgy efforts, compounded by highway engineers' devotion to straight and true. Much of the world is like Mr. Lazy Pants down the street's fixer bike. Seeing it makes me shudder. I want to pull over and finish the job. With a little effort, it could be a tolerable It'll Do Bike. A block later, I no longer care.

"Think of it as a test," Marta answered. "How resilient is your brain?"

My route is not remarkable, at least to me, because I've been there, done that. I will not be fording rivers, visiting primitive tribes, sleeping in fields, or riding dragon tails. It doesn't include a Must Do Bucket List Motorcycle Road.

Do you think Magellan and da Gama felt titillated 100 percent of the time? Try 5 percent. They filled their Nothingness Sea miles with keelhauling, flogging, slave girl canoodling, and plank walking. Do you imagine training always blew Usain Bolt's mind? No, he ran for the brief payoff that came when he crossed the finish line. Road trips are not endless curves, exotic landscapes, track races, or never-ending world wonders. You must hone patience. Failure to flush and restore your perspective leads to throttle aggression. You think, I'd rather be in the back seat of a car playing Halo. Or switch on autonomous drive. Take a nap or have sex. On-motorcycle, you can't do any of those things. All you have is your perspective—better take care of it.

"Send updates," SQUID Dolores requested.
"Be scientific," Conrad said.
"Keep the hustle to a minimum."

There's a lot of embellishment in the biker community. It's okay because it flows from the joy of the machines.

"My updates will be factual," I said. "Just the revolvements."

Marta winked.

Scrape Your Lists, The Motorcycle Files

Should your mind start to ping, nagging for the definition of a strange capitalized word used by the Tony's gang (and in all Scraping Pegs books) to express our motorcycle adventures (like NimRod or Blockhead) or a term (like Motorcycle Narcissism), check out *Scrape Your Lists, The Motorcycle Files*. It has answers and is a curvy, titillating read on an unusual road. It's motorcycling, expressed in point form.

Now, Let's Get Going!

PART TWO: THE RIDE

6

The Send-Off

More than ten thousand people were involved in the prep work. Can you imagine hundreds of millions of global spectators applauding your departure? Waving, *Good for you! Way to go, modern-day explorer! Tweak your state of mind, friend!* We understand: the wheels are round and they roll. That sort of thing. It would be Fuckin' Fantastic with two capital Fs.

Celebrities appeared. One thousand seven hundred fifty humans and two hundred horses paraded.

"Good gravy!"

"We should be chomping English pasties," Cameron said.

"Anything but their fruitcake."

"Mince pie?"

"Battenberg cake?"

"Very elegant," media hosts proclaimed.

We were at Tony's. I'd ordered a Tony's Cinnamon Roll and coffee. Conrad and Den split a Cosmic Special. Manny had the Tart of the Month. Dolores and Earl ordered pastel de natas, the Portuguese egg custard pastry. Anita and Ben had coffee concoctions.

"Be better if the motorcycle escort was more prominent," Conrad pointed out. "And stopped regularly to do stunts." A rerun of an English monarch's coronation was playing on TV.

We agreed.

The ruler of England was making a quick trip around the palace neighborhood

"Good grief," Elena, Tony's assistant manager, said.

"Should have ridden for the event," I said. The royal horse, alone in a stable, missed the jubilee extravaganza. For sure, we would have watched longer had the spectacle included a monarch on horseback, enduring the Ass Problem. Practicing balance. Exercising control. Doing the wave. Still, we marveled at the sense of purpose.

"Born into other circumstances, they'd be on our team," Marta declared.

In London, at the time of the jubilee, the royal procession director was thrilled. Millions of viewers. Love and admiration.

"It's hard to picture some members of the royal family as gearheads."

"Perhaps on trikes?"

"Circling home base?"

"But a nice people."

"What d'you think about adding Bedfordshire clangers to the international menu?" Tony asked.

My send-off wasn't as grand. There were no royal cannon salutes. No rifle regiments. Not a single fireboat sprayed water. No lap dancers squirmed. No one fired a starter's pistol. No cheerleader squads formed hanging stags. Not even Mayor Dumbass, who pops up for all photo ops except biker events, showed up.

In our garage, as I made final preparations, Dori didn't attend. Marriages—loving ones—teach the value of silence.

I circled Neuro like a pilot focused on his preinspection. Checking Neuro, I wondered, What have I forgotten? I've learned not to fret. As long as I have tap-to-pay, I'll survive.

When the time came for me to head out, Dori appeared. "Bye," she said with the hint of a smile.

"Bye," I replied, and we hugged.

For a moment, we deeply missed each other. But, as it was for Shackleton, once the mooring ropes are hauled onboard, you are adrift. There's always a moment of doubt.

Without fanfare, I climbed on. Up went the garage door. Before me was **Get Out of Dodge Lane.** Down the street I rode, a Loner-By-Choice. As if I were going to buy a jug of nonfat milk for a royal tea, the media paid no attention. Not a single neighbor lined the street.

A solitary crow chawed.

People adore monarchs and celebrities, making them feel blessed each time they venture out. I felt alone and ignored.

Marta says, "Motorcycle brains are like wheels. Gotta roll for a bit to settle them down."

I made the first left. Riding solo is the way to roll when you're in need of a tune-up. It's like buying a good quality degreaser rather than struggling with soap, cheap cleaning products, water, and those high-tech rags. Solo dodges the equivalent of lashing your old lawn mower and gutless vacuum cleaner onto your tail bracket and riding to Service as a trio . "Here you go, Dr. Tire. Tune my motorcycle up, please." Meanwhile, Vacuum and Lawnmower jabber on about malfunctions affecting their trivial utility. Dr. Tire scratches his head. What's going on here? There's a trio of machines. How can I focus when they're in a pack? By the way, is your vacuum grey or gray?

Riding with buddies is great, but if you're out to recalibrate your brain, uncluttered is best. As a lone voyageur, you must nudge yourself to get on with the endless tasks that move life along. There is no following the pack. Without a group mentality, your perception leads the way.

When you travel in a group, thoughts like, why doesn't the lead bike go faster, fester. How come Pete brakes in every corner? My god, Mary looks delicious on-motorcycle. What's up with the intercoms? We're stopping in this shit hole? The really tall guy needs a different bike. Wonder what they'd do if I tore off? Clutter like that.

Most motorcycle travel books lead off with a revelation. We wish our solo explorer God's speed. We pray the rider will find peace before the end of their very interesting trip. Occasionally, the rider is doing something out of the ordinary, like touring on a tiny scooter. We get it! We understand there is MAGIC in the soul of your machine.

All I had was a tune-up directive coupled with Marta's vague raison d'être assignment. *Shouldn't I be on a real quest? Like Anthony Hopkins in The World's Fastest Indian?*

Marta says: "You can make any ride interesting. If you consciously pay attention to your ride, your journey will shape who you are. Every trip can be monumental."

I had my doubts.

Confession: part of me didn't want to go—thanks to my ambulance ride with my motorcycle pants cut off and wearing a neck brace. The threat lingered on my mind. Mucky fluids congeal, clouding your brain with trepidation. Fortunately, the kid voice in me grew loud and shouted, Gotta Go! Gotta Go!

Off we went to visit Santa Claus. Climb on my lap, biker-boy. Thanks, no. But here's the list of farkles I want. By the way, I saw the Big Bad Wolf chomping on one of your reindeer.

"Don't be a weenie. Climb back on," online advisors wrote after my accident.

I did, gingerly, a year after Horace. But I'm not the rider I once was. Mikey Boy died on Highway 20.

There was no hoopla on Get Out of Dodge Lane. A crow flew off. A dog barked. And just before the turn, there she was—Strawberry Ajello, walking her mutt. That was it. I waved, but Strawberry didn't. Biker-idiot, she probably thought, without knowing it was me. My dog Pearl and Strawberry's rat dog are buddies. I sometimes think about asking Strawberry if she'd like to go for a ride. Want some MAGIC? Ditch the mutt and hop on.

People reserve cheering for media darlings, royalty, world record holders, Nobel Prize winners, and those going to Mars. *Oh well.* The lack of respect for short motorcycle getaways is understandable. Had I been on three wheels, I'd at least have had the curiosity factor. Is that a motorcycle with too many wheels or a car missing a tire? What's it all about? Intriguing. A short getaway, you say? Please tell me more.

"Loads of room on your three-wheeler," I imagined Strawberry saying.

I sat alone on Neuro with culinary gold—a Tony's Cinnamon Roll, one Tart of the Month, and two Cosmic Special sandwiches, which come with battered pickles. A send-off fit for a king!

After the first left, there was no going back.

Forward the Light Brigade!

My Motorcycle State of Mind: Charge!

I was off home base, heading for first.
Decked out in a brand-new Tony's tee shirt.

Looking forward to eating half a bun on the ferry and my first big challenge—the One Nacho Rule—is it possible to stop at half a bun?

Of course, I could have gone around the block and stole home. English monarchs parade through the neighborhood and then return to the palace.

I imagine, had the ruler been on-motorcycle, they'd have rode to Joy. Screw Buckingham Palace! Let me show you where majesty really lives. Let's ride up to Balmoral and give them the finger, shall we?

As Conrad says, "It'd be a real shit show if everyone wanted to be a monarch. Or if everyone had to win the lottery. Or everyone chained themselves to a tree to save the planet."

Marta's raison d'être assignment was over-the-top. Nothing like Anthony Hopkins trying to set a land-speed record in *The World's Fastest Indian*. But I'd try to pound a wobbly stake in to keep my friend happy. If it topples over, no problem; there's nothing wrong with leading a life that's not purposeful as long as you're able to get out of Dodge occasionally.

Yes, I'm making progress on my revolvements, my reports to Marta will say.

7

Road Vomit

It wasn't long before I ran into Road Vomit. Before Motorcycle, the term was "the doldrums"—stuck on windless waters with a ship full of conscripts and rudimentary facilities. The Tony's gang says,
No wind. No problem!

It's a reminder to be thankful we were born After Motorcycle.

Exploring today requires a different mindset. The conquest of earth by humans is not in question. Before Motorcycle, Captain Cook, Chris Columbus, and the rest sailed on pristine waters—no traffic, signal lights, horns, road rage, exhausts, or climate change. Today Vomit is everywhere, causing motorcycles to crawl like wounded ants. Neuro suffered in urban despair. "Hold on, buddy. We'll get through this." The signal changed and into the swarm of red taillights we went.

I sat over a hot engine in direct sunlight wearing grey and black armored clothing. My gear was breathable, but nothing breathes when you're a snail perched over a hot engine. Urban density suffocates riders—cagers are smart to shelter in cars.

Eventually, the hooting, belching, shimmering traffic lurched forward to the next junction and again stopped.

There can be grace within the hideous frankness of cities. But it eludes motorcycles ambushed by the human condition. Bikes must move and cities have no sympathy or benevolence. We wait beside cagers relaxing on enormous seats, adjusting their climate controls, dining, watching TikTok, and sending tweets. They look at us and think, biker-idiot.

Urban Vomit expands the way fatties add mass. Obesity settles in and grows beyond reason. The city where I live is trying to grow fat like Chicago or London or Kuala Lumpur. It hasn't reached *Falling Down* levels yet, but that seems to be the goal of our dumbass politicians. More. Bigger. Better. Grow the GNP and the tax base. Expand and build our way to utopia.

In the movie *Falling Down*, actor Michael Douglas, stuck in thick LA traffic, becomes unhinged and goes on a rampage. Road Vomit can push even comfortable cagers over the edge. Automobile amour can't contain it.

As Neuro passed through the city's center, I imagined myself as an old-world explorer contending with troubled waters. Push through, or everything is lost. Batten the hatches and heave to! Then I missed the light change thanks to the NimRod ahead of me. Clear sailing soon, I promised Neuro, and managed to keep from blowing a gasket.

My Motorcycle State of Mind: Close to the Boiling Point.

"Until you're clear of traffic lights and intersections, your trip isn't underway. You've pushed away from the dock. Not yet out of the harbor." That's Marta's thinking. "Guarantees a good start," she explained to SQUID Dolores.

At the Black Ball Ferry terminal payment booth, I tapped my phone. Don't leave home without it. Let me tell you, being credit-card-less is horrific. No different from an explorer sailing toward the edge of the earth without fermenting fruit and vegetables. The cost is scurvy. Gums rot and spew putrid black blood. Gangrene sets in, forcing sailors to use their knives to cut into flesh and discharge a foul liquid.

Some years ago I forgot my card—it felt just like that. So I called out: "Biker in distress!" The Motorcycle Commandment kicked in: No member of the brotherhood/sisterhood shall be left behind.

Riders have an obligation to assist bikers in distress. When I found myself without means, I leaned on my Motorcycle Friends. (I wasn't with my close buddies, so it was awkward.) Like perpetually running on empty, I always felt vulnerable.

Exploitation, rather than help, was the fate of explorers of old. The buccaneer code of conduct was "fuck you, mateys." After Motorcycle, exploring became civilized.

By the time I'd pulled into the ferry lot, I'd knocked off two road trip reminders:

1. The trip doesn't start until all Road Vomit is cleared.
2. Complete two credit card checks.

Gassing up the day before is #3, but it's not a mandatory. Completing the checklist preps me, like a NASA astronaut hearing, "T minus zero. All systems go." I ignore the part about being locked in a pod without a smidgeon of therapeutic value, at the mercy of a fireball, thinking, is it too late to call in sick and ride a motorcycle instead?

I stopped beside a group of motorbikes. Neuro's kickstand went down. I looked up. It was picturesque, as downtown parking lots go.

Nine driver-bike couples were waiting to board. Two-wheelers (and three) are segregated from four-or-more-wheelers and bonded by a shared passion. We introduced ourselves.

"This is Neuro. We're heading south."

"These are my new riding boots. What d'you think?"

"Do you carry a 10mm closed? I need to tighten a nut."

Stuff like that.

Following an exchange of chitchat, I began profiling.

"Don't judge a biker by their helmet," Marta says.

But when I share my observations, she pays attention.

I tagged the gentleman next to me, Alexander the Conqueror, for, according to him, he'd conquered all things motorcycle. "I live with my bike all summer long." He'd been down every road everywhere and possessed an encyclopedic knowledge of the "best bikes," "best roads," and "proper riding techniques." He informed me my new helmet was okay, but I should have purchased the white flip-up full-featured model he wore.

Joining Alexander was Cleopatra—the couple formed a motorcycle relationship of convenience. At age eighteen, the original Cleopatra wed her brother Ptolemy XIII to become queen. Later, she seduced and married Romans Julius Caesar and then Mark Antony. This Cleopatra was bolted to Alexander. The couple wore identical helmets.

Riders and bikes fall in and out of love. I suspected the young biker next to me was disgruntled. Something as natural as a flat tire or fouled injector can lead to machine-biker conflict. The young man was pouting. Perhaps he wanted to travel two-up but was rejected? Perhaps his preload wasn't dialed in? He wore a scratched, run-of-the-mill black open-face helmet.

All the other owner-machine combos waiting at the ferry terminal were enthusiastic couples.

The man three bikes over was lustful, smitten by the Coolidge effect, enamored with his shiny new machine. He stroked its young novel, unblemished steel and paint. The allure of low miles and new rubber. His helmet had a decal on it.

Every group has a Phaedrus, the *Zen and the Art of Motorcycle Maintenance* dude. Overly analytical and, at times, disenchanted. They always wear plain white well-used helmets.

One guy, with a black half helmet, looked like Hannibal ready to kick ass. Stay out of my way!

"Very few of us are what we seem," Marta says to counter my profiling hobby. "I may be the anomaly. Guzzi and I are an open book. An exact match." Marta owns several helmets.

She and Guzzi are a match like Cinderella and Prince Charming. Or Lady and the Tramp. Valentino Rossi and his YZR-M1. Lennon and McCartney before Yoko.

Corralled, our bikes were in a protective formation, waiting to board. Like a wagon train in the Old West, snug and comfortable in our community. We enjoyed ourselves until a loudspeaker instructed us to disperse and join the pre-boarding passport check queue.

I surveyed the border control lineup—how many dubious types would stall my progression, my return to Neuro?

One woman resembled the recluse from Charles Dickens' masterpiece *Great Expectations*. In my mind, I pictured her wearing the same frumpy white dress all the time, like Miss Havisham, the spinster who never changed out of the wedding dress she wore when her groom abandoned her at the altar. My Miss Havisham also traveled solo, possibly jilted by her lover. She looked out-of-the-norm, which made her a target.

Immigration officials would pounce and drag her through the interrogation process to flatten their monthly racial profiling statistics. *Are you a witch? Do you seek revenge against American men? Why didn't you pack more clothes?* Stuff like that.

I wanted to embrace Miss Havisham to revive her trust in relationships, but the authorities would note my kindness as Suspicious Behavior.

Further along, two Ahmed Ressam types waited to be called. This pair was lighthearted, with an obvious hint of the Gotta Go spirit. That wasn't the case on December 14, 1999, when Ahmed Ressam was arrested by US Border Protection. He was attempting to enter the United States via the ferry I was about to board. Authorities uncovered homemade bombs with timing devices hidden in his car.

Ahmed and his conspirators wanted to blow up Los Angeles International Airport on New Year's Eve. A rampage like in *Falling Down*, except triggered by religion, not Road Vomit.

"Ride is always the answer. Not bombs." Marta's right, of course.

One good thing about motorcycles. Terrorists never bomb them.

"Passport," the officer said. I handed mine over like a pro, opened to my picture. The explorer returns!

Border agents profiled me and asked the prescribed questions. I was careful not to appear shifty, deceptive, or over-the-top. It's impossible to know what border guards are thinking. No facial expressions, especially grins and smiles. Frank Serpico scanned my passport and paused, waiting for the computer to respond. Serpico returned my passport, giving a thumbs-up.

My official was Serpico, from the based-on-actual-events movie. I wanted to ask Frank if he was in on the Ahmed Ressam bust, but the border rule is: "We ask all the questions. Do not speak unless spoken to."

US officials screen Coho passengers in a small office on the Canadian side. When called, you step forward. No funny business! Hand over your documents. Remain silent. Provide only requested information.

If you've seen the *Seinfeld* "Soup Nazi" episode, it's exactly like that.

I've crossed the border many times. The cloud computing brain has me slotted under *Harmless Jackass*.

"Proceed." I stepped smartly to the side.

A slight nod is acceptable. But never "How's it going on the southern border?" or questions of that nature. Frank wasn't likely to be a biker—people who give society's laws and norms the finger are screened out.

Back with Neuro, I worried about Gulliver the Traveler. He'd flown from France to LA, where he purchased a used Harley for the "veritable experience Americana." Gulliver had an outlaw appearance but spoke like a teddy bear with a French accent. He planned to return to LA, sell his bike, and fly home. His passport was full of stamps, each representing a motorbike trip.

I knew Frank Serpico would slap him down like a tank bag.

As we were about to board, Gulliver jogged back. Exasperated Frenchmen are hilarious. I changed his profile to Inspector Clouseau. Clouseau nearly qualified as a rider in distress. That would have been a real pain in the ass.

"Balade," I said. French for ride, I thought.

Presenting tickets, passports, identification on a motorbike requires practice and a plan. What to do with gloves? Where to stash paperwork, money, wallet, credit card, phone? I'd honed my system over the years, so I completed the task without incident as we drove aboard. SQUIDs fumbled, dropped, switched engines off, and checked pockets.

I'm a ferry pro—very familiar with how to secure your pride and joy, tying down and blocking a motorcycle. I assisted perplexed rookies in distress. Do it like this. You'll find more blocks over there. It goes on the other side, Ferry SQUID. Stuff like that.

Helping Motorcycle People, especially know-it-alls like Alexander the Conqueror, I figured was my revolvement obligation done for the day. I sent a text to Marta—"No doubt riders on the Coho have me profiled as Gearhead Mahatma Gandhi. A great start to my trip."

8

Ride The Ferry

In 1959, when the MV Coho made its maiden voyage, it carried BSAs, Electra Glides, Nortons, R50s, Japanese bikes, Royal Enfields, and an Oddball Ural. With a capacity of 110 vehicles, the private ferry is tiny and ancient compared to government ships. She's a trooper—like those workhorse bikes that never quit.

Forced to abandon our cherished machines lashed in the belly of a windowless iron crate, bikers rose from the dim belly of the Coho. On deck, we were passengers, deferring to a captain who ensured there would be no exploring. Twice daily in the summer, once in the winter, the Coho steers a fixed course between Victoria, BC and Port Angeles, WA.

Motorcycles bolt out of driveways and proceed with grace onto the car deck. When the Coho pulls away from the dock, every steel beam groans as if the ship is loath to be underway. The hull crackles like the driest twigs under the tires of a dirt bike. Water is pushed aside as the boat parts the ocean, bound for a foreign shore to deliver its precious cargo.

On this day, the ocean remained calm and our spirits were high. The boat would not take deep dives, the kind that rattle riders who fear for the safety of their machines. I've been on heaving, huffing, pitching ferryboats and wondered, *Is the boat trying to destroy my bike?*

Sir Ernest Shackleton had horses, and dogs clinched to the decks of his ships. It only got worse for the few miserable creatures forsaken by man and God, who reached the shores of Antarctica. Imagine your beauty battered and thrashed on an open deck in horrible weather, washed by sea salt, and then dumped in front of a crusher on the shore of a distant wasteland.

The great mass of the Coho steamed on, holding a direct and certain course for America. The rushing water was as plainly heard as the wind is on-motorcycle. "Ride the waves!" sailors say.

"No thanks," say Motorcycle People.

Ferries and bikes don't mix well. We're creatures of motion; ferries trap us in limbo. We don't wait well—especially parked between RVs and semis with kill markers. Bikes relish the freedom to stray off course, while ferries are bound to timetables and fixed coordinates. They're stuck in a rut. Motorcycles? They slip the leash. Veer, pause, reconsider. They write their own route in real time—freedom isn't on a schedule.

We found comfort in being amongst our own. Most of the gang assembled outside the coffee bar, keen to avoid a moment's pause in our road tale conversations. A shared vigor energized each member of our party as we waited to dock and release our bikes from captivity. I peered out at the vast ocean as Sir Ernst would have—not a speck of pack ice in sight.

Time to toast my departure with a cinnamon roll, I thought, but I was reluctant to take the sharable sized bun out in public. Instead, I chose the smaller, more sophisticated Tart of the Month.

9

Fountains

A gentleman shuffled along, nervous the mighty Coho might shift, roll, and chuck him overboard. Down ships go, sucking passengers into their vortex, pulling them under, filling their lungs with water. The tradition is: captains go down with their ships. Motorcycles do not have a history of bondage. One machine has MAGIC; the other collects barnacles.

The old-timer wasn't looking further than his next step. Worried about fracturing a hip, he did not dwell on the possibility of the Coho flinging him into the watery abyss. His bones were frail, but the gent had a glint in his eye and a twinkle in his voice. "Fountains of Youth, your bikes. They keep you young. Yes? Always wanted a Harley. Glenda, the Mrs., couldn't picture this"—he motioned, indicating his body—"as hell on wheels."

"Young at heart, perhaps," Stu, standing beside me, answered.

"Sciatica," Motorcycle Dreamer said, thumping his leg. "But I manage. Glenda thinks not, but I could do it. A Harley ... it'd whack a few years off." He snickered to conceal his doubts. "Never too late, right?"

"No reasons not to ... but start small." A tricycle. I smiled at the modern-day Ponce de León, the Spanish explorer who searched for the mythical treasure. It's like the **first ignition of a new bike—hope wrapped in combustion,** available with a turn of the throttle—wind and motion, the magical elixir.

A Fountain of Youth poster hangs on a wall of my garage. Marta inserted the word MOTORCYCLE. "Bikes foster childlike wonder.

Climb on and be a kid again." Too bad Ponce was born Before Motorcycle.

"Best be getting back," Motorcycle Dreamer said. "The Mrs. will be waiting ... worried the old boy took a tumble." He chuckled. "Ride safe."

"Think he'll buy a Harley?" Stu asked as the man shuffled off.

"Not a chance. What with the Mrs. and his sciatica."

"He has the spirit. It's a shame... he never spun the wheels."

The two of us sat on one of those hard bench seats ferries love. We sipped coffee and chatted about age, Dreamers, and procrastination. The trips we hadn't gotten around to. The bike we always wanted but never bought. That sort of stuff. I took out Tony's Cinnamon Roll and offered Stu a piece. Politely he declined. I figured he would. But how can you resist the aroma of the gooey spice?

Stu was also an uncertain returnee. "Rode dirt since I was a kid. Quit riding a few years ago. Had my fill. Then I started thinking about touring."

I remembered switching from dirt to asphalt. It's a significant life event. Like a bar mitzvah, catholic confirmation, or your first orgasm.

"I became consumed with the notion of buying one of those big-ass road bikes," Stu said. "Do a one-eighty. To hell with trails! Ride in comfort. Explore far and wide. Aside from short rips on barely legal bikes, I've never taken a road trip. The prospect excited me. Which bike to buy? Where to go first? So many roads." Full of road trip anticipation JOY, Stu was a boy again thanks to the Motorcycle Fountain of Youth.

"Lots of great choices. Which way did you go?"

"That dream is on hold... for now." Stu was heading to Washington State to ride Hurricane Ridge.

"You got an adventure bike?"

"KLR 300R trail bike. According to my longtime riding buddy, Klaus, a tolerable compromise. 'If you must ride asphalt.'"

"Folks cross continents on Honda 90s," I reminded.

"Not me. My dream was a fat-ass tourer with all the bells and whistles.

Strictly pavement. Seen enough dirt."

"You can explore on any bike," the Marta in me said.

"Klaus kept pestering me until I made the compromise. The KLR will do pavement. Short day trips. My buddy doesn't know, but I made a deal to trade the KLR in on a tourer, if I choose. One more month to decide. I may be at the end of my dirt days." His grin was that of a child after pulling a prank.

I pictured my new Motorcycle Friend caught by a press gang. Before Motorcycle, many sailors never chose to go. The Royal Navy and other European nations used harsh methods of forced recruitment. Three or four men would seize candidates, shackle them, smack them on the head if needed, and drag them off. Welcome to your sea adventure, buddy!

Today, motorcycle sales professionals know customers want to come aboard. Transform their image. Become weekend warriors. What's a few bucks when you can drive off and start a new life, pal? But Stu's friend had pressed him to buy a bike that wasn't his dream machine.

"'Don't be a Half-Biker,' Klaus says. He figures if you can't go off-road, there's no point."

I nodded. One of those. Cam used to be like that.

"At some point, I conceded and bought the dual-purpose."

"But you have an out?"

"Yes."

I took a bite, politely put half of my bun away, and waited for Stu's story. He was at a crossroad.

His Motorcycle State of Mind: Switching Gears.

<u>Stu's Motorcycle Story</u>

Klaus watched the suspension rebound. He's one of those who understands damping, unsprung mass, and notions that are the domain of service and enduro tracks. In his early fifties, the man looked years younger than Stu but was two years older. "Doesn't age," Stu told me.

Klaus was a keen backpacker. Allegedly he enjoyed sleeping on a thin pad in a tiny tent, besieged by mosquitoes and threatened by storms and wildlife. Years ago, the friends rode, parked their bikes, and hiked into remote camping spots. Not something Stu wished to repeat.

"Enough dirt." He'd had enough. "Road bikes stop at motels." Klaus called it, 'accepting half-measures.'"

"Nothing wrong with a comfortable saddle and a bed at night," I assured Stu.

"Coast downhill to your grave or stay off-road. Your choice," Klaus would say. He's a take-no-prisoners kind of guy."

I pinched a piece of bun from under the wrap. *Are you familiar with Templar Knights?* I profiled Stu's friend, in the Middle Ages, mounted on a warhorse, part of an advance shock troop charging at the enemy to smash opposition lines. Take on prisoners. No half-bikers!

The friends met at the Pear Lake trailhead for what Klaus called Stu's dirt test. "Still in you buddy. No need to become a half-biker." Klaus had pedaled his bicycle to the trailhead.

"Sorry. Have to bail, bud. First ride and all. But go. Take it easy. Get to know your new wheels without distraction." He stepped back. "Work ... know how it is. Next weekend for sure. After your shake-down."

I was reminded of Marta's words: "Sometimes the best help you can give someone is to leave them alone. Go solo. Be self-reliant."

Stu had nodded. There won't be a next weekend. And today I may cruise up Old Mill Road instead of the power line cut.

On his dream bike, it'd be no contest. Comfortably roll over to Benson. Grab a coffee and a breakfast sandwich. He'd answer questions: Yes, you don't see many DB5Rs in these parts. No one notices trail bikes. Even Motorcycle Dreamers don't care about dirt.

"Whatever you do, don't stop before the lake—beautiful and loads of great track on the way. Take your time. No grandstanding! "No cell service after mile one. You don't want to have a problem out there ... on your own. You don't, do you?"

Stu shook his head. *Won't be an issue on Old Mill Road.*

"Incredible lake. You'll see. I've hiked in and camped. Piece of cake on a bike." Klaus fist-bumped his friend's shoulder. "Best get moving.

Enjoy your ride, bud." As if apologizing, he added, "Something to be said for solitude ... in nature, beside a perfect lake. Revitalizing. You wouldn't get that on the road."

Horse shit! Ride, then nap on a Perfect Sleeper. Now that's *restorative.*

Stu told me, "Despite it all, I really wanted to pass my dirt test. Leave like a pro, not wimp out, you know? When I was younger, I used to ride like I was on fire. ScareDevil Stu, they called me."

The trail followed a power line through seventy-three miles of hill country toward Benson. It had a locked gate with a weathered, neglected NO ACCESS sign. Explorers with fearful hearts might look at the barricade and turn away. Stu had pushed KLR to the far side, ready to pound it out to Pear Lake. "My last ride on dirt."

As he stretched, sweat collected at the base of his neck. It wasn't just a ride; it was a turning point. The end of an era. Even more emotional than changing motorcycle brands or styles. It's like getting divorced, changing jobs, or realizing—I identify as a bagger, not a trail rider.

"Don't try to hit a home run," Klaus had said before pedaling away.

Scant forest and scrub flank each side of the cut. The lake is short of halfway to Benson. Wildflowers take charge of clearings in May, growing nature's perfect garden. After a few bends and dives, ScareDevil emerged. No fear! Feather the throttle. Yabba dabba doo! Ride, Stewie! Ride!

"The KLR seemed less agile than my previous bikes. Or perhaps it's me? Almost three years older."

The KLR had accelerated out of a puddle, spraying water to the sides, then ran through a rut. On a smooth stretch, the engine revved, lifting the front wheel off the ground. Klaus would have hollered, "Wild man," but JOY, not Klaus, was Stu's guide now. Mile after mile, he raced. Then slowed when thicker pine forest replaced the low boundary of the scrub country. Here and there, monumental outcroppings of rock.

"There was no end, as if the path ran beyond the horizon."

"I know the feeling." I wondered if I shouldn't take a dirt test. Return to dirt? Off-road with Cam?

Crouching, Stu had ducked under a low-hanging branch. Nature's booby trap. Get the hell out of here, biker! But the ground, bathed in white flowers, welcomed Stu's machine.

The wheels dropped into a rut. ScareDevil stood on the pegs; his low-speed skills solid.

Street bike? What was I thinking? "I felt ten years younger."

A root grabbed the front tire and tugged hard right. Automatically, Stu's foot went down. KLR recovered. Klaus's warning replayed—the worst thing you can do alone is injure yourself.

Don't be a wild man! Found ravished by wolves. Ravens picking at eyeballs. "We're not invincible! Don't bust your collar bone again!"

The bike slowed and pulled over in a spot where the trail widened as if expecting oncoming traffic. Stu flicked some of the wet mud off the front fender with his glove. He could see the singleness of intention, the honesty of the engineering—humble but unmistakably capable. He couldn't picture trading the KLR in now that he had christened it. "Two bikes," I thought. "May be the answer."

After a sip of water, Stu climbed back on. The machine purred under him, solid and agile. It broke and ran, leaped and crouched, swerved and dodged, then slowed. Less elegant than a DB5R, but a capable explorer.

As my new Motorcycle Friend talked, I wondered if Shackleton had formed a bond with Endurance? Columbus with Pinta? Pounce with Santa María de la Consolación?

"Then shoulder bursitis pounded a dull ache." Stu tried not to lean on the handlebar and gripped the throttle gently. How much further? Every bump had threatened to launch a firestorm.

Cautiously, the KLR advanced, and the shoulder settled down to a low-grade, nagging reminder—we all age. The bike rounded a corner and there it was, Pear Lake in full view. Dark emerald green. Ringed by rocky cliffs and wildflowers. Trees reflected on the water's surface.

The kill switch restored silence; birds resumed singing the praise of nature's majesty—the amazing work Mother Nature tucks away in spots unseen except by Templar Knights. Stu stood, his right arm hooked in his jacket like Napoleon.

There should be a sign: **Brought to You by Motorcycle! Your Fountain of Youth.**

"Sorry," Stu apologized for intruding, but it was unnecessary. Motorcycles can rocket and disturb, but they have their place. Stu wasn't at the helm of a whaler wishing to harpoon Moby Dick's children; he was passing through, as birds do who soar above cities.

What about the lesser creatures? Stu wondered. Bloodsuckers in the lake. Centipedes and other loathsome vermin along the shore. Snakes in the grass. If you have to be an animal, be a bird. If you must be a machine, be a motorcycle.

The warm air made Stu's riding gear feel thick and heavy. The jacket came off. Now dive under, he thought. Cut off from everything, immersed in the cool greenish liquid. But the vegetation on the far side of the lake looked prehistoric. The forest behind the lake, impenetrable. Do Not Disturb, it said. Klaus would have barged in like a Templar Knight.

Stu nudged the KLR forward and then checked his viewfinder. He turned the wheel a plug length. *Click.* Another photo over here. *Click.* Thanks for bringing me!

"That's the moment when I stopped thinking of the KLR as a loaner," Stu told me.

He took the tank bag off and sat on a log, eating dark chocolate almonds for lunch. Klaus would have had a fresh veggie plate with quinoa. Across the water, an eagle perched on a tree branch. *Waiting for what? For how long?*

"It's OK," Stu told the predator. "Leaving soon. You'll have your lake back." He wasn't there to raise a flag, slaughter, or enslave.

KLR swung around and rolled down the trail without gunning its engine. Now the ride was automatic. The machine knew the trail and chose the best track. No need to study throttle, brake, gears, balance—it all just happened. Stu wondered: Could the first ride on a big street bike come anywhere close to this? Must it be one or the other? Dirt or street? Young or old? Is there a dividing line?

On-motorcycle, everything is under control until it's not. Stu pumped the front brake, forcing the bike to a wobbly stop. He stooped to inspect the tire—flat.

"Fucking fuck!" He booted the wheel. Punctured.

He checked his phone—no bars. Still at least five miles out. He considered driving, sacrificing the rubber, but it was too rough and the dealer might renege on their trade-in deal. "Return it in like-new condition." He longed to be sprawled on a Perfect Sleeper, with a luxury tourer waiting outside his door.

The route back was more down than up, and the bike rolled with little effort, as if begging, Please don't abandon me. But as Stu trudged on, it gained weight.

"Pick me up with your trailer," Stu demanded when there was a cell signal. "I'll be at the trailhead in less than an hour." He knew Klaus would be chuckling. The Templar Knight would have jogged out and then marched back, toting everything needed to fix the flat. Piece of cake!

The crippled bike stood strapped down on the deck of Klaus's trailer. Obliterated by a flat tire and shoulder pain, Stu's composure was gone. He could sense sacs swelling with fluid, fueling inflammation, driving shoulder pain.

"You okay?" Klaus had asked.

Pounding. Throbbing. Pissed-off. *What'd you think?* "It reminded me why I'd given up riding off-road," Stu told me. "Dirt's a young man's game."

"How was it… after two years on the bench? And Pear Lake? Overlooking the flat," Klaus had asked.

Stu glowered. "Sucked." It's how you deal with a tough-as-nails bike snob.

Klaus didn't react. Takes time: bikes are like mountains—peaks and valleys. "Next weekend, Cotter's Trail. If the weather's good, we'll camp."

Stu shuddered. *How 'bout Old Mill Road on a well-padded seat?*

"Up for Cotter's Trail?"

"If my shoulder's better." Spoken like a boy complying with his father. "No camping!"

"No lake, but a terrific view."

Probably have traded the KLR in by then.

"Stretch. Omegas."

"Need a new tire." While Klaus explained tire tread, Stu turned KLR.

At home that night, he deleted pictures of the street bikes he'd had his eye on. He selected a photo of KLR in front of Pear Lake for his home screen. He couldn't say why, but the vision of the lake and the memory of the ride invigorated him. His shoulder had settled down. The sound, of time, tic toc, tic toc, had waned.

Instead, he heard YABBA DABBA DO! Ride ScareDevil, ride! "Maybe dirt is a sort of fountain of youth," Stu said.

He sent a text to Klaus: "9:30, good for Cotter's Trail?"

Stu chuckled and shook his head. "Knew you're no half-biker, Klaus told me. Just the same, I'm planning a road trip."

* * *

On the Coho, I thanked Stu for reminding me of the great days I'd experienced off-road. "Good luck with your decision."

"Think I'll know, for sure, after Hurricane Ridge. Once I'm home."

I spoke of my accident and how my riding had evolved. "Better to adapt than to stop." We traded numbers. "Let me know how it turns out." Perhaps we'll tour together? A pair of road warriors who once played in dirt. "My friend Bob used to tell me 'you need at least two bikes.' Three works best."

Stu nodded. "Sounds right. One would be big-ass. Comfortable. Tire thread made for pavement. Maybe with a drink holder?"

"I may pick up a small dual-purpose ... next year," I said.

Probably not.

Motorcycle Dreamer returned with the Mrs. "What do you say, Glenda? Buy one of those three-wheel bikes? What do you recommend, boys?"

A loudspeaker cut in with an announcement: we were nearing our destination.

* * *

As we stood by our bikes, waiting to unload, I recalled how a scrap with Diego Columbus, Christopher's son, had interfered with Ponce de León's Fountain of Youth search. As well, he'd been ordered to establish a Florida colony. Life distracted him. He passed at age forty-seven.

"You'd think," I recalled telling Tony's gang, "someone believing in the miracle of eternal youth wouldn't let anything distract them. Why didn't Ponce say fuck you and go all in on his search? What could possibly be more important?"

"He was a Dreamer," Conrad had answered. "They never go all in."

"Fountains leak," Den said. "Sooner or later, we all notice the years dripping away."

"Had Ponce been born later, he'd have discovered motorcycles. Would have put him on the right track," Earl said.

"Forget fountains. Put gas in your tank."

"Maybe try monkey nuts," SQUIB Dolores had suggested. She'd been reading about Dr. Serge Voronoff, who performed the first monkey-gland-to-man-testicle xenograft in 1920. Voronoff suspected that transplanting monkey glands could suspend human aging.

It can't. The doctor gave up after experimenting on hundreds of aging volunteers over the course of a decade.

"Ride," Marta proclaimed, "Is the fountain of youth for those who discover the secret... how to maintain a balanced Motorcycle State of Mind."

The Coho slowed. Helmets and gloves went on.

I mulled over the term Half-Biker and sent a message: "Marta, I've decided my raison d'être is to not be a Half-Biker. Another revolvement: I'm going to ride dirt again!"

Probably not.

I could hear Marta telling Tony, "Nowhere near being balanced yet."

I added: "There may be a good deal on a KLR 300 coming up."

"Mikey Boy rides again?" Tony would say.

A couple of weeks after my road trip, I received a text from Stu. "Took a Concours for a test ride. With panniers and top box. It was a little disconcerting. Felt top-heavy. Not used to so much machine."

It's unsettling, switching from dirt to road. Like having a foreskin snipped off or getting a mastectomy.

"But once I got rolling, it was great. No bursitis!"

10

The Road

As the shoreline drew near, there was much speculation about the best roads to travel.

"There's a turnoff here."

"No, go further and take Fairy Lake Road," Alexander the Conqueror insisted.

Phaedrus checked his map. Fairy Lake Road?

"We're going to grind it out to the 45," the Harley pair said.

Stuff like that.

Alexander had waypoints mapped out with interval timings. He assured Cleopatra "keeping to our schedule will avoid rain." Go here, not there. Do this, not that. All constraints of his making.

The Tony's gang likes to say: Don't mind the weather if the wind don't blow.

SQUID Dolores says it's an example of innuendo. "Detour if there's a bump in the road. Otherwise, ride on."

"Alright," I responded when Alexander told me what my best course of action would be. "Thanks." There is no debating with his type.

The rest of our group was wondering, Where might we find ourselves tomorrow, the next day, in a week, and so forth? I said little. I like to drift. It's impossible, with certainty, to foresee where tomorrow may find me. I don't expect flawless. Disruption is part of my journey and it may place me on an unintended course.

"Down the coast," I told Inspector Clouseau once Alexander moved on. Clouseau would stay on the interstate all the way to LA and then home to France.

Suddenly, there was a violent assault; the sound of the hull grating on timbers. Worse than new side cases grinding against cement. Our camaraderie dwindled as we concentrated on readying our machines and ourselves.

The Coho stopped rasping, panting, and snorting and hugged the wharf. Pleased to be chained to land, the engines fell silent, replaced by a trumpet of motorcycles preparing for liberation. Every eye pointed in the same direction. I nodded to Stu and pulled my gloves on. Dreamer gave the thumbs up. The Mrs. looked displeased.

How beautiful and free! The motorbikes. Then we saw earth below us, not steel nor water.

Pioneers built old Port Angeles on a hillside looking out over the Pacific. I suppose they watched for sailing ships and whales.

Up we went until the earth leveled. Most of the traffic headed east toward Seattle, the interstate, and the continent beyond. Neuro turned west onto a sparsely traveled highway. Soon the Port Angeles Road Vomit dwindled and I sang, ♪The magical machine is rolling now, and every single breath I draw is Hallelujah◇.

My Motorcycle State of Mind: Hell a Fuckin'lujah! Ride! MikeBoy, ride!

So I poked the throttle, and away we went.

Later, I reported to Marta, "Glad to be on my way. Loving it!"

"Freedom on the road, the cliché of cruising into the sunset—simply doesn't exist." I remembered Dori saying that just before we stopped riding two-up. The notion offended me at the time. How can you not feel the wind? The liberation?

Not everybody does. Some prefer yoga or swinging beads.

I once went with my neighbor to a WLC Harbour Cats ball game. The Ass Problem attacked while I sat on a plank in the stands, pretending to be having fun. I waited for what felt like an eternity, all the while dreaming of returning home. Off-motorcycle activities are often like that. Marta explains, "Once you're used to moving, being present on-motorcycle, it can be tough to sit and wait things out."

Now on the open road, I felt blessed to feel the call of the next bend. The sound of nature combined with a myriad of moving parts and synthetic rubber on asphalt. Everything running right. Some autopilot, muscle-memory part of my brain commanding micro movements and maintaining two-wheel balance. My mind running through memories and what-ifs, playfully and at times intensely, triggered by something I passed or by nothing at all.

My brain was busy discarding trash.

What the fuck? A deranged red light brought traffic on the two-lane old-school rural highway to a halt. On the far side, a hill with two quaint, craggy peaks stared down upon the misplaced signal. Why are you here, beyond the city limits, without an intersection? Are you a prankster? Have you gone rogue?

My Motorcycle State of Mind: You've Got To Be Kidding Me.

Move down the endless highway, not stop on it.

Is there no escape from vomit?

Breathe. In. Out. In. Out.

Marta would say something like, "Take the opportunity to stretch. Observe your surroundings. Chat with a fellow traveler. This is an opportunity, not a delay."

I was on the verge of a Falling Down rampage, but, as signal lights do, the light turned green. Go! Off with you. Thank you for respecting my need to take control.

"Get a real job," I swore at the light.

The reason for the stoppage? A single-lane detour around a modest road construction project. Neuro followed seven cars into a dip over a seal-coated surface. The road gently bent around a disturbance. At the detour entrance, a sign declared: **Motorcycles Use Extreme Caution.**

There were no directives for other types of vehicles. It booted my inclusivity state of mind in the plugs. The detour was neither rutted nor hazardous. SQUID Blockheads could ride through it. So why single gearheads out? On principle, I refused to use extreme caution and emerged fine, thank you.

But all was not well. Thanks to the light, I was at the tail end of a parade of seven vehicles, all of us bound for a twelve-mile stretch of superb curvature where the 101 snakes alongside Crescent Lake.

Repositioning before the lake run was critical. I had to be in the lead position before passing became illegal and dicey. What would Neil Armstrong have done had Columbia encountered Russian Sputniks blocking his moon shot? He'd have fired all rockets.

My Motorcycle State of Mind: Race On! But in cautious post-crash governor mode.

It was imperative Neuro be in the lead before reaching the lake. We pulled out and revved high at every opportunity. Biker-idiot, car drivers cursed, but what do they know? Cagers believe motorcycles must use extreme caution where it isn't the least bit necessary. And they believe twisties are an engineering disgrace.

Old-school road builders respected the graceful contours of Crescent Lake's shoreline. They embraced rather than bulldozed. Their restraint produced a remarkable stretch of pavement. The renegade engineers delivered a message: Fuck cars! We built this for you, motorbikes!

Leading the charge, Neuro blasted through the first series of bends. The lake chortled and bubbled with glee. The force and resistance of physics whistled, Ride like the wind, Mikey Boy. But don't be a Blockhead! Remember, shit happens!

My Motorcycle State of Mind: Guardedly Twisted.

Along the lake there are torrents of warning signs, placed at coordinates specified by modern-day risk management specialists. They say things like:

SLOW TO 25 MPH
SPEED LIMIT 35 MPH

NO PASSING
SHARP CURVE AHEAD
NO PASSING
SLOW

Inevitably, Neuro pulled up behind a slow-moving NimRod intent on obeying all instructions ad nauseam. There are no passing opportunities along Crescent Lake. Virtuous drivers pull over. When I pass I wave, Bless you, Cager Saints!

The selfish dawdler forced me to throttle down. "Pointless to get bent out of shape," Marta would say.

To distract myself from the wasted curvature, I peered out at the large body of water. A lone fisher sat in an open boat. Catching trout is an extreme test of patience. I took my cue from the forbearance of the fisherperson.

Ride with JOY, even when selfish cagers block your way and refuse to pull over.

I successfully switched my **Motorcycle State of Mind to: Gone Fishing**.

At the end of the lake, after pulling over, I sent an update to rub in my glory to those left stranded at home plate.

While I was enjoying the remains of my cinnamon roll, Marta replied: "A good idea for a road sign would be **Motorcyclists, Proceed Like Fishers**."

Then Conrad suggested, "Drive Like Cheetahs."

"Soar Like Eagles."

"Gear Down Like Elephants."

I missed my friends, but gloating is a terrific distraction.

11

Gas Stop

Trees, thousands of trees, immense monsters reaching tall; at their feet, ferns and vines hugging the soil — and then no trees at all, where humanity had raped the forest. Saplings, they're called, the signs of rebirth, but the ancient forest will never return.

On-motorcycle, conflict and struggle are apparent. Riders are in constant motion; it's a blessing to ride away from the human condition. Motorcycles cannot be logging trucks or slave ships; on-motorcycle, you must be respectful.

For miles, no houses, no sheds, no decay. Asphalt and the solitude of two wheels. Nature can make Loners-By-Choice feel small, like a single beetle crawling through the undergrowth.

Huge trees now bordered the road. I was in a rainforest, the air heavy with the smell of moss and damp bark, an earthy rot that threatened to erupt. I looked for a sign—Motorcycles Use Extreme Caution! Mother Nature may attack with both barrels! You're a sitting duck!

"How dare your kind rape my forests?" Mother asks. "I seek revenge!"

"Piss off, Mother!" I'd done my homework and was confident Neuro would pass unmolested. The forecast called for overcast with those sprinkles that are too weak to penetrate motorcycle wind currents. Not too hot. Not cold. Perfect for riding.

The Tony's gang says, pay attention to meteorologists. They're not just reading the news.

An hour west of the ferry terminal, I reached Forks, Washington, the wettest town in the contiguous United States. Annual rainfall averages 120 inches (for comparison, Glasgow receives 54 inches, New York City 50 inches, Paris and Victoria 23 inches each). Author Stephanie Meyer set her vampire-romance cult classic, *Twilight*, in wet and eerie Forks. Vampires are severely unbalanced, incapable of riding due to their obliterated mindsets.

Playing it safe, I decided to gas up in the next town.

At Forks, the 101 turns to follow the coast south. Rivers, mountains, deep green meadows, and craggy rocks flank the highway, often dark with trees. At times a fine mist washed over Neuro—the ocean pressing: Pay attention to me! Over here! Look down from the sky to the sea. We are never-ending, constantly shifting from peaceful to playful. The salt mist misted my visor. It tasted metallic, like the sweat of the ocean.

Miles passed. I was happy moseying along without knowing why.

My Motorcycle State of Mind: Content, like a dog getting its belly scratched, or a cat stretched out on a bed.

It's a delight to be alive, on-motorcycle. My whole being seemed to be one with the surroundings, the dull sunlight, the odors, the engine, the comforting calmness of the universe on a superb day. Mind you, my thighs ached just enough to remind me I need to step off soon.

The ride from Port Angeles had been hypnotic—road noise a low chant, tires humming on asphalt like a monk's mantra. Then it shattered. Then there it was. Human debris strewn on a stretch of pavement.

We dodged garbage tossed from an automobile. I've never come across motorcycle litter.

* * *

Read a few motorcycle books and you learn that magical encounters at out-of-the-way gas stations are commonplace. Behind the crumbling service station lives a motorcycle sage. He hears the throaty notes of a bike pulling in and ambles out. Behold, a wizard, weathered, wise, and content. The enlightened one shares a wealth of knowledge.

"It was a fortuitous turn of events for me," the contemplative traveler writes. "Early in my momentous trip of self-discovery."

So there was an air of expectation as I pulled up to the pumps outside the village of Queets (population 200). Across the road a sign proclaimed: **Home of The World's Tallest Spruce Tree.**

Had Cam been with me, he'd have insisted, "Let's get a photo. Our bikes in front of a world record giant."

"The tree's not a GPS point of interest. I don't want to go on a hunt."

"It's tall; we'll see it."

"Too tall to capture with the bikes in a photograph." *So why bother?*

Had Cam prevailed, the gang at Tony's would have seen our tiny bikes in front of a tree slightly taller than its neighbors.

"What method was used to determine it is indeed the tallest spruce on the planet?" engineer Marta would ask.

"It'd be like trying to verify weapons of mass destruction."

"Looks like a fir. Sure it's not a fir?"

"Is there a food truck parked close by? To make the stop worthwhile."

"Be kinda neat to pee behind a world record holder."

Comments like that.

The Queets station fit the motorcycle sage scenario to a tee. Out of the way with character galore. What lurks within? What is its history? What pearls of wisdom will be bestowed upon me? It made me giddy with anticipation.

My friend Den is an encyclopedia of popular music and says the Beatles happened "out of the blue. A miracle really, like discovering pneumatic tires."

On July 6, 1957, fifteen-year-old Paul McCartney attended the annual Woolton Parish Church Garden Fete. He hoped to meet a girl. He may not have found a sweetheart, but he heard a high school band, *The*

Quarrymen. The lead singer was John Lennon. The two boys lived in different neighborhoods, went to different schools, and were two years apart in age. But because Paul stopped at the church, the Beatles happened. The Beatles reinvented music.

I looked forward to meeting my John in the village of Queets.

It was a no-name self-serve pump well past its prime. *Fill your jalopy here, not your sophisticated highly tuned engine.* I hesitated, but then pumped, listening for approaching footsteps. Nothing out of the ordinary happened, so I strolled into the run-down shop attached to a single-bay garage. I carried my helmet and wore my motorcycle jacket. I was the equivalent of a decked-out NBA star dropping in on his hometown high school tournament.

There could be no mistake about my mission; I was about to be blessed by royalty.

The place smelt of boiled cabbage and oil rags. I looked for motorcycle memorabilia but saw none. Not a hint of a classic restoration or an artful chopper. No posters or racing trophies. I waited for my all-knowing sage to appear—John, get the hell out here!

It was melancholy, like a business that had taken to drinking and lost its way. A layer of dust burdened with grease lay on every surface. Wear had created holes in the battleship linoleum. The washroom was dirty and foul-smelling; I flushed, using my boot. The toilet moaned and farted. Fearing the overflow, I fled.

Behind the counter sat an acne-scarred adolescent. The boy looked like Mark Samuelson from my eighth-grade class. If I had to guess what was showing on Mark's face, I would have said hopelessness and resignation. But perhaps there was an underlying spirit of adventure. A thirst to explore.

Was it the surroundings that colored his appearance? Stuck in a sageless decaying box?

"Hello," I said smartly, and for good measure, "Cool for this time of the year, but great riding weather." *Is your uncle a motorcycle sage? When do you expect him?*

The boy didn't stray from his phone.

"I imagine the big spruce tree is enjoying the weather." Still nothing. "Lived here long?"

A nod, but otherwise Mark didn't move from his pale reality. He lived in a narrow region of blind phone resignation, never to be uplifted. There would be no moments of anguish or JOY. He kept his foot rooted to home plate. Perhaps he'd get up to Forks, but never consider the South Pole.

Mother Mary in Heaven, Mark! Use your damn phone to search for a small dual-purpose bike! Perhaps Stu will sell you his KLR. Here's his number. Get on with it! Explore, lad, explore!

I suppose it's not easy to move out from under the shadow of the World's Tallest Spruce Tree.

Neuro carried me away. My sage wasn't in Queets—too wet for motorcycles, I suppose. I'd likely find my John further south.

***

As the wheels rolled, I imagined what it would be like to grow up as Mark. Motorcycle-less. Trapped by a smartphone inside a decaying gas station without a sage. To the north, a community of vampires. Further south, redwoods mocking spruce trees. Stuck at a fossil fuel station as EVs drove by.

Just as Ahmed Ressam had planned to bomb LAX, full of *Falling Down* rage, one day Mark would blow up the World's Tallest Spruce Tree.

It had to be done to break the chains.

The boy would fill his uncle's chainsaw with gas from the old pump and then reduce the overgrown tree to manageable chunks.

Huge Firewood Sale would replace **World's Tallest Spruce Tree.**

Mark would use the revenue to buy a mid-sized motorcycle. Then the boy would escape. Head east, toward the flatlands where trees are not oppressive and motorcycle sages flourish.

These observations full of clarity, only happen on-motorcycle.

"Marta, a revolvement!" I wrote. "I may move to Queets. Become a motorcycle sage. Setup a hotdog stand under the world's largest spruce tree."

12

Little Big Horn

I am a man of flimsy excuses. Rather than ridiculing folks like Mark, I should concentrate on planting my stake in the ground. Find my raison d'être.

If I fill the gaping sage hole in the Pacific Northwest, I'd cheat, using my phone to connect to the Tony's gang for real-time support. Help! This young man seeks the secret of trail braking. As a sage, I'd need more than "it's a feel and can't be described."

To diversify, I'd have Tony invest in a second-hand food truck. Also hard-sell fridge magnets and coffee mugs along with the world's tallest hot dog and battered pickles to finance my sage duties.

The problem? I would make a lousy sage. I'd hide behind the garage, reluctant to emerge, pissed by the growing number of bikes passing by while I'm stuck being a stationary sage.

Putting a stake in the ground isn't going to be easy, I decided as Neuro rolled south. I may give up; being persistent is difficult when you really don't care because you're a free spirit, on-motorcycle.

Sir Ernest Shackleton was a man who got on with it. He had tank bags of fortitude when it came to exploring the South Pole. Stranded in Antarctica for four hundred ninety-seven days, he survived on provisions recovered before Endurance sank. Dog meat for dinner helped his crew sidestep death. Sir Ernest never faltered.

I will not eat my dog Pearly and can be pushed off course by run-of-the-mill events. Unlike Indiana Jones, my resolve would have hightailed it, had my beloved TS-125 dropped into a den of snakes. Snakes wrapping around Suzuki's wheels and slithering up her frame? Mother Nature in Heaven, save me from your wretched demons!

As I put Queets in the rearview mirror, the heat from a single sun ray reminded me of our vulnerability and the time Global Warming ambushed me in Death Valley. It reduced me to General George Custer, in the wrong place and up against tremendous fortitude.

I'd already ridden many miles before turning onto Highway 190 bound for Lake Havasu, where a Motorcycle Friend waited. We'd met at a rest stop a year earlier. Our relationship was a convenient Gotta Go excuse. "It'll be great to meet up with good old Lar again," I had told Dori. I had my doubts, as you do with folks you don't really know, but I was eager to go.

His name was Larry Baar, but I profiled him as General George; a heavier, easygoing George Custer. The person the general might have been, had he been born After Motorcycle. "Let's ride," he'd have told Crazy Horse. "Avoid Little Big Horn altogether. No need to make a last stand."

I rode toward Arizona with nothing more interesting to look at than my GPS, which was stuck on "We're not making progress. Quit looking at me, Jackass! Why didn't you stop at the El Cheapo Motel and Ice Cream Shop? Continue in the morning's bearable heat? Are you trying to melt me down? So what if Larry-We-Hardly-Know is waiting? I don't care!"

I'm more OCD than outlaw when it comes to appointment times.

Pack ice is sluggish. You can nap on the deck while it inches along. It won't freeze or fry your neurons. Death Valley Global Warming is much faster, quickly overpowering motorcyclists, turning motion into a blowtorch while melting down GPS circuitry.

Hundreds of awful miles, each meter a blast furnace slog. My head baking inside a helmet that had promised to make the difference between a comfortable ride and a suffocating one. Hour after hour of Motorcycle Misery. As I passed through Shit Hole Junction, I looked around and wondered, Why does anyone choose to live in this godforsaken place? What am I doing here? Who the hell is Larry Baar, anyway?

I don't care!

I sent Lar a text advising I may be a bit early.

I often remember trips like Lake Havasu. The times when reality and Mother Nature triumphed, made a joke of the search for balance and adventure. Made me wonder which auto dealer would take my bike on a trade.

The truth is, there are times motorcycles rattle riders. "Piss you off," Conrad says. "And rattle your state of mind," Marta admits.

I stuck both feet in Lake Havasu's water and Lar handed me a drink. General George turned out to be a merry man. In the course of a beer or two, he restored JOY. His *Worst Rides Make the Best Stories* tales had me hooting. Unlike the Battle of Little Big Horn, you can quickly recover and move on from Motorcycle Misery. Lar and I rode north together on back roads, steering clear of Death Valley.

My brother Ron, The King of Bullheaded, looks like Ernest Shackleton. Ron wouldn't stop walking until he reached the South Pole or perished. I share his relentless gene, but mine is compromised. It wants to stop at the Cozy Penguin Inn. I'd complete the second half of the expedition in one of those enclosed heated snow track buggies, preferably with a beverage service. Hey Ron, I made it! What's the difference how I got here? I arrived bang on schedule!

I understand Gas Station Mark's thinking. Never stray; I may get trapped in pack ice or fried by the sun! Something bad may leap out of the forest and crush me. I may plunge into a pit of snakes. The cell signal bars are strongest here, inside the station.

Stay put, Mark. It's okay. Weenies Matter! You're under no obligation to climb on. You're safe on home plate.

At Mark's age, simple urges consume boys. Watch pornography. Steal a Snickers bar. Buy some gummies. Get tanked. Stuff like that. The kid was years away from needing a responsible raison d'être. When Mark's time comes, an AI app will show him the way.

I'm past the point where basic instincts supply holler-from-the-rooftops motivation, yet I putter along fine without a pebble of meaty inspiration on my bones. Remember my tee shirt?

I Don't Care!

It didn't matter until Marta decided it did. Thank you, Marta, for spinning my head like an unbalanced wheel! For making me fret—now my neurons feel obligated to steam to the South Pole. As can happen on-motorcycle, out of nowhere came a brainwave. My raison d'être would be to Never Give a Shit (bikes excluded). I'd have to wrestle with my appointment time obsession. Also, the honesty of pie, the gooeyness of cinnamon rolls, the well-being of my family and pets, and other stuff like that.

Life for me is a compromise. Like traveling; Alaska is doubtful. Kiruna in Lapland perhaps. Reindeer are known to be helpful, and Conrad has ancestors in the area. If his relatives will put us up and lend us their Husqvarnas, why not?

Neuro pulled up behind a truck. It's bumper sticker read:

You Got a Big Bick.

I moved forward to see the small print. **Did you read that wrong?**

* * *

On one side, trees similar to the size of the Queets spruce. If Cam were with me, he'd insist on stopping. "We may have found a new champion. It'll get us into the Guinness Book of World Records."

"Cam, I don't care!"

Rolling hills, rock formations, and rich green thickets replaced the massive trees. On the other side, the contrast of sand and ocean came and went. The gas stop was distant now. On-motorcycle, there is a profound sense of moving on. Wheels are round and they roll, we say at Tony's. Asphalt blurs. Life changes.

13

Magic Carpet

I remembered SQUID Dolores relating the book *One Thousand and One Nights* to her first road trip. "It felt like gliding on an enchanted carpet—it lifts you, smooths your edges, and carries you somewhere new. It's the motorcyclist's version of Aladdin's Lamp: the wheels spin, and suddenly you're elsewhere, mind cleared."

In the story, Aladdin discovers magic and a flying carpet. "Motorcycles are modern-day flying carpets, except on-carpet you fly above the road."

It's a nice way of looking at things. It was the start of Den calling his nephew, Morgan, the Magic Carpet Kid.

We encouraged him. "What the heck has the Magic Carpet Kid been up to, Den?"

"Flying," Conrad always answered.

An eagle swooped down and then shot up.

Morgan's Motorcycle Story

Even at a young age, Morgan had two-wheel fever, according to Uncle Den. He tore around endlessly on his dad's old KTM 125, a bike Den had passed down to his younger brother. It wasn't pristine: the front fork leaked, the clutch was hard to engage, the tires were bald. "Never hear the boy grumble," Den told us. "Nuts about riding." All deficiencies were excused, including the ill-fitting hand-me-down body armor.

The KTM was king until Morgan turned sixteen and said, "Dad, I'm ready for a larger bike."

Mr. Kent occasionally got the itch and rode the KTM. He was taller and much heavier than his son. "You just think you need a bigger bike. Uncle Den rode the 125 for years."

It had to do with matters beyond transportation; teenagers have impulses parents once understood. "An adventure bike, neater than the KTM. Maybe a GS," Morgan told his uncle. "Something I can ride to school." Impress the sweethearts. What Uncle Den called a bad-ass naked bike, like in the movie *Rebel Without a Cause*. James Dean cool.

Morgan's mom, the sensible one in the Kent family, barely tolerated the KTM and had a line in the dirt. "It's one thing playing in the field, but you will not be riding in traffic as long as you're living under this roof, young man!" Morgan's father never challenged the decree; he understood Riding Rule #1: Everyone is Trying to Kill You—his wife's declaration was undeniable.

The message went in one Morgan ear and out the other. Yeah. Yeah. Yeah. He was impervious. "She'll come round," he assured his best friend, Larson. Kids learn how to win parents over. Persist. Manipulate. Never be deterred. Learn how to pull strings.

At fourteen, Morgan had made several clandestine five-mile road trips to Larson's house on the unlicensed and uninsured KTM. He and Lars had a story cooked up in case his dad arrived home unexpectedly, perhaps from an "extended lunch." Mr. Larson was the devil when he drank.

Incognito meant Morgan could not use his "no one tried to run me off the road" rationale on Mom.

"Mom can be such a NimRod," he told Lars, using the word learned from Uncle Den.

"A good way to get yourself killed or crippled," Mom repeated whenever the street bike subject came up. Stan Jankowski proved roads and bikes don't mix. Stan had lost control of his Yamaha ten miles south of the Kent house. Now he limps and talks weird. "Look what happened to Mr. Jankowski."

"Dana's never forgiven me for giving my brother my old KTM," Den told us. "Motorcycles don't make good presents."

Den's brother knew Stan the Man, but he'd kept his opinion about Mr. Jankowski being a Blockhead to himself.

"What does Mom know? Jankowski never rode a dirt bike," Morgan told Dad. "Uncle Den says dirt bike school can't be beat. You said Mr. Jankowski's not even a good butcher."

Stan always looked disgruntled working behind the chain store meat counter. His eyes had a look of contempt. He carried his fat paunch without modesty on his stubby legs. "Mr. Jankowski is the kind that rides with the idea of showing what he can do, which is less than he realizes. It's a bitter lesson."

Morgan nodded. Exactly. "A Blockhead."

"It's not an argument you'll win with Mom." Mr. Kent had given up thoughts of buying a touring bike and hitting the road with his brother. He'd once tried to convince his wife it'd be fun to ride together, but was pointless.

Morgan turned sixteen without convincing Mom. *I possess skills most riders never gain—dirt bike immunity.*

"Bet Stan Jankowski figured he wasn't in harm's way."

But I've ridden to Larsen's many times. Nothing happened!

Adult opinions frustrate the hell out of teenagers. But at seventeen, destiny opened a door. Dolores called it, "Aladdin finding magic in a cave."

"Out of the blue," Den said.

It was an old, poorly customized black Virago. Stored in Mitch Brenner's parents' garden shed. It had shorty ape hangers, a crudely fitted sissy bar, and cheap nonstock pipes—the 500cc V-twin version; four times the displacement of the KTM. Viragos sit low. After a test ride, Morgan boasted he could pick quarters off sidewalks. A high school senior, Mitch was dumping the bike to go to university out of town.

"Not what I'm looking for," Morgan said. There was no panache. It was the kind of motorcycle Mrs. Flanders might contentedly ride each day to her job at Cowley's Concrete Forms. It was not the bike a hot-blooded teenaged boy wanted to be seen riding. The Virago looked like a bike that was trying too hard, totally devoid of sparkle. And without the sparkle, you might just as well avoid the rain, cold and discomfort and drive a car. But he asked, "How is it at two-up?"

"Snuggle machine. Girls love it," Mitch promised. "The ladies aren't into muscle and tall dirt bikes. This is what they go for. Low and comfortable. Movie bikes."

Girls adored Mitch. He'd experienced things Morgan dreamed about. "Mitch knows his stuff," he told Lars.

"Trust me," Mitch said. "If you want some action, this is the bike for you."

Like a genie, Mitch made motorcycle ownership feasible—a bike with a proven history of attracting cheerleaders. Arms around me, instead of Mitch, Magic Carpet Kid dreamed. It was cheap, which is essential when dipping your toe in and working part time at Burger King.

"We could put the stock handlebars on and take the sissy bar off," Larsen suggested. "I'll kick in for gas … when we're two-up … till I get my own bike."

The Virago stayed in Mitch's shed, waiting for Morgan to break the news to Mom. *I paid for it with my own money. You won't have to pick me up anymore. It's not a rocket and cheap on gas.*

Whenever a motorcycle story popped up on the news, Mom said, "Just like poor Stan Jankowski. See, Morgan? Against cars, bikes always lose."

"Mr. Jankowski wasn't hit by a car, Mom."

"Against trees and asphalt … they always lose. No protection on a bike. Ask Stan Jankowski."

"Dad?"

"My brother just shrugged," Den told us. "Job one is keeping the peace."

For the first month, Morgan had worked on the Virago in Mitch's shed. He told Jeanie Swanson he was fixing up his new bike. "Used to belong to Mitch. Getting it ready for the road. Then I'll take you for a spin?" She didn't say no, so Morgan had a sense of urgency, especially now that it was looking better.

"Can't keep it in the shed forever," Mitch said. "The ladies won't wait forever."

"Soon," Morgan promised.

"Where's your bike?" Jeanie asked.

"So, Morgan told Dad his secret and my brother broke the news to Dana."

"Be thankful our son isn't shooting up or getting pissed every weekend. Den's ridden for years. Nothing bad happened to him. Never had an accident."

"What about his friend, Mike?"

The couple didn't speak for days.

"It was tense," Den told the gang. "A no-win situation."

"A bit like the booby-trapped cave Aladdin faced," SQUID Dolores added.

"Too good a deal to pass up, Mom," Morgan explained. "Had to move quick or lose it. No choice."

"Ride it in the field … like you do on Uncle Den's old bike."

"What?" Morgan looked at Dad. *Is Mom nuts?*

"It's a street bike," Dad explained. "Needs pavement."

"Get your money back from Mitch, then."

"Final sale."

"I'll call Mitch's mom."

Kids know how to sulk and make parents feel bad, compelling them to come round. "There'll be limitations," Dad said when they reached a truce. "Road safety training. Listen to your Uncle Den."

"Be happy the bike isn't a Panigale or M1000RR or FXDR 114," Den had told Dana.

"Stan Jankowski," Mom said. "No riding after dark. No speeding. Any trouble and that bike's history!"

"Truth be told, it wasn't much of a bike," Den told us. "I'd have advised Magic Carpet Kid to pass on it."

Morgan caught himself listening to each erratic beat of the engine. *Is it about to die?* It's a sober truth: the first purchase of an inexpensive used machine can be a bitter lesson. The last flickers of life unloaded on a naïve SQUID.

But the Virago rolled on. Surprised, Mitch said, "You got yourself one hell of a deal, Morgan."

Sometimes Morgan picked out an object ahead and concentrated on making it that far. The boy measured the Virago's progress in baby steps, gradually becoming accustomed to its complaints—noises, sputters, and relentless death threats.

The morning had been altogether devoid of enthusiasm. Overhead, the sun blazed thanklessly through the depleted atmosphere. Dogs sought shade. Feet dragged. Flowers drooped. So, this is life?

Then there she was. Jeanie Swanson. Standing in the Central Pharmacy parking lot. The spitting image of the iconic Marilyn Monroe poster. Morgan could feel her sitting behind him, leaning forward. Those tube-topped breasts pressing against his back. Her hand on the back of his neck rubbing and then those full lips of hers. Ride to the woods! The music playing: ♫All I wanna know is, sexy, can I? Can I◇? When she stepped off the bike, her jeans down low on her hips showed lovely light-caramel-colored flesh. ♫Can I? Can I◇?

<u>Morgan's Motorcycle State of Mind: Two-wheel sexy.</u>

A goddess. A beacon of what is possible. God signaling the way. Or perhaps Mitch had left some of his magic with his old Virago?

"Boy, did Aladdin rub the lamp," SQUID Dolores said.

Morgan had swung his magic carpet chick bait around and pulled in. When he hit the kill switch, the engine ran on for a couple of seconds before it died.

Jeanie looked unimpressed. She thought Morgan should have got a red bike like her cousin's. She reached over and yanked the Virago's mirror—it didn't budge. Morgan beamed.

"So, this is it?" Jeanie asked. "Not a Harley?" It wasn't as nice as Larry Sullivan's Lancer.

"Used to be Mitch's ride. Had her up to a hundred." Down Pine Tree Hill. Morgan handed Jeanie the outdated helmet Mitch had thrown in for the promise of a free Whopper. "Hop on. Let's go for a spin."

But it wasn't a Harley. And Mitch wasn't driving. The helmet became a hot potato—Jeanie wasn't sure what to do with it. Her friend, Adelina, nudged her. "Go on. I'll wait. It'll be fun."

"Hold on," Morgan yelled as the engine fired up. He'd drilled holes in the pipes to make the sound sweeter and up the power profile.

"To what?"

"Me, silly."

Jeanie wrapped both arms around Morgan's waist.

Mitch nailed it, Morgan thought. "Ready?" *For the woods?*

"Go slow! And stay in the lot," Jeanie shouted.

"Don't worry." Dirt bike immunity. He eased the bike into gear and they took to the skies on a magic carpet.

Jeanie felt Mitch's nasty helmet messing up her hair.

Adelina waved.

"Neat, hey," Morgan called. Jeanie's fingers pressed into his stomach. She couldn't understand a word. "Why's it so loud?"

"Your turn," she told Adelina when they stopped. "It's fun." She handed her friend the stinky helmet.

"Better not. My brother had one. Scared the piss out of me." Adelina gave the helmet back to Morgan.

"What kind of bike?" Morgan asked.

"White," Adelina answered.

Morgan nodded.

"Let's get a pic," Jeanie said, straightening her hair. She passed her phone to Adelina. "Me first."

Morgan forwarded a selfie with an arm around each girl to Larsen.

Motorcycles make dreams come true.

Two days later, on his way to Lar's, Morgan spotted his goddess in the front seat of Rob Horton's primer-grey Hyundai. Adelina sat in the back seat. Rap music blasted from the custom sound system. ♪I feel like a rap god. Rap god◇.

The Virago didn't have a sound system, just pipes with holes.

Adelina recognized the Virago, stuck her arm out the window, and waved.

The Virago turned right and sputtered away. At Larsen's, Morgan muttered about needing a better bike.

"Already?"

"Never planned to keep it long. Maybe a Jeep ... with a sound system. Mom will kick in."

Morgan stood outside the Burger King before his shift, looking at his bike. Too small and not enough chrome. An Electra Glide with Cobra pipes and a music system? Or a carbon-black ZX-10R? Add a few farkles and Jeanie would be swept off her feet.

A month later, the Virago sounded as if it needed a transplant and soon died. Morgan glared. Mitch suggested, "Sell it for parts. Probably worth more than you paid."

It wasn't.

"I had a look," Den updated us. "Dead. No doubt about it."

Dad had hugged his son. He knew the anguish of machines turning to junk.

"Hunk of shit," Morgan told Larsen.

Lars nodded. He'd always thought so.

"Next it was a used but newer Suzuki Marauder," Den said.

"A safer bike," Morgan had assured Mom.

"It is quieter."

"Different bike?" Jeanie asked. "Or did you paint your old one?"

"Newer."

"Shinier." Adelina seemed impressed.

Magic Carpet Kid beamed.

A few days later, the Marauder pulled up beside Adelina. Morgan was on his way home from Burger King. "Like to go for a spin?" Adelina, with her bronzy radiant skin, wore those big hoops and had her hair pulled back. She held a Schwinn bicycle and was evolving into a fossil-fuel-hating vegan. "No, thanks."

"Another time." Morgan smiled. He couldn't figure the girl out.

As for Jeanie, it was clear that she preferred cars.

"Not everybody is swept away by magic carpets," SQUID Dolores said. "When you're young, it's impossible to figure out why everyone doesn't think like you."

***

Of all gifts, perseverance is preeminent; it toughens and molds character. Time passed. Morgant Kid brooded—quiet desolation mixed with the immense exuberance of early adulthood.

His Motorcycle State of Mind: Down In the Dumps.

"Morgan went back to tearing around on my old KTM," Den said. 'Take your time,' I advised. 'Don't let the absence of owning your own ride bother you.' I saw he was out of sorts. Girl trouble."

A year after high school graduation, Morgan bumped into Jeanie. She laughed when he reminded her about their parking lot ride. When her face muscles contorted, his goddess appeared strikingly plain, not at all like Marilyn Monroe. She said she was expecting and engaged to Rob Horton. "Look for an invitation."

"Went through half my twenties bike-less," Den said.

"And not getting any," Earl joked.

"Like wandering in the desert," Marta said.

"Life interferes."

"Aladdin set aside," SQUID Dolores said. "Growing up."

Then one day Den reported, "The Magic Carpet Kid's back in the game." Morgan had rubbed the lamp.

"Both Morgan and Lars bought Kawasaki Ninjas, sport bikes doing duty as tourers." Den showed pics of the young men and their bikes parked at a viewpoint.

At home they attended Bike Nights, where Morgan met Macy. "She rides a V-Strom. Very nice young woman," Den told us.

"Like a stream of light through the heavens." SQUID Dolores sang her colorful words.

Macy introduced Lars to Solange, who mentioned she had always wanted to ride a motorcycle.

When Mom met Macy, Mom asked, 'Do you know Stan Jankowski?'"

Good lord!

"They make a beautiful couple … or foursome, with their machines." Proudly, Uncle Den showed pictures. "The kid's thinking of trading the Ninja in on a KTM 890."

We agreed it would go well with Macy's V-Strom.

**

Hearing about people fortunate enough to find Motorcycle Compatibility is heartwarming.

According to SQUID Dolores, "They rubbed the magic lamp and could fly."

Much different than Gas Station Mark. As I rode, I worried Mark would never find his perfect match. Few cheerleaders pull in to fill up at shabby pumps in the woods.

I dialed Neuro up to Jabber Killer. *The boy didn't even say hello, for Christ's sake. Why worry about him?*

Gas stations are spots where humanity connects. Then people drive off. Motion dissolves lingering thoughts; on-motorcycle they become impalpable and frivolous. My mind cleared. The I Don't Care state of mind became entrenched. It's possible because, unlike magic carpets, motorcycles are real.

My Motorcycle State of Mind: On a Magic Carpet Ride.

I sent a note. No explanation necessary. Marta would know exactly what I meant.

I leaned forward and let Neuro scream. A speed limit sign appeared. We conformed and then broke the cager's laws. We slowed, and I rocked the wheels. Whatever I wanted to do, I did.

At a viewpoint, Tony's Cosmic Special, including a battered pickle, came out of my top case. I stood beside Neuro, gazing out at the immense ocean. I imagined Sir Ernest sailing south. He waved; I know, Ernest. I know. You gotta go! Me too!

Something that looked like a carpet flew beyond the horizon.

I bit into a battered pickle. Holy Mother of fermented scrumptiousness!

14

A Bridge

The uncertainty of what will be seen next is powerful. On-motorcycle life and its environment bombard you. Feedback loops create a model of who you are, allowing you to form a perception of the world. "Next time you feel trapped by your reality, climb on," Marta says.

Will there be more of the same? Or an abrupt change; a freak of nature, a manmade oddity, wildlife, an odd cloud formation, an ambush, or indescribable beauty? You must sweep through the curve. Straighten up to check for the unexpected. Every curve reveals a fresh view.

What waits down the road can be repetition or perhaps a racetrack. At times, my viewfinder operates on Energy Saving Mode with only my road radar running effectively. I look, but nothing distracts me. No discernible features. I look but I do not see. Sometimes my brain needs a swift kick in the neurotransmitters.

I came out of a sweeper and in the distance saw a creature-like shape at the edge of the forest. "Holy Sasquatch!"

My body rose as I pushed on the pegs, and the wind carried away my involuntary, triumphant shout. I was Sir Edmund Hillary, looking down on Earth from the top of the world. Marco Polo, astonished by treasures found along the Silk Road. This was it! Every explorer's dream. Discovering life on Mars or a timid Sasquatch down the road from the vampires in Forks.

The hairy giant's arm moved. Will it attack? Are they like deer? Or defensive of their territory and anonymity? I slowed, uncertain about my next move. Accounts of hairy wild man-apes stalking these parts stretch well beyond the footprints and grainy photos that bewilder scientists. Believers wait for years hoping to glimpse the elusive Bigfoot, and here it was. Made possible by the MAGIC of motorcycles. He stood beside the road, now only a football field ahead. He was perfectly still, both amazed and disturbed, as the indigenous must have been when they first sighted European sailing ships off the coast of North America.

You lucky bastard! A motorcycle, not a sailing ship carrying disease, lust, domination, and damnation.

When I got closer, I saw my Sasquatch was a tree stump with its roots torn out of the ground. I sat down and sulked as Neuro passed. It was apparent something traumatic had happened to the tree. That it had suffered a gruesome demise. But there are many trees in the forest. Who cares? I hoped to sight something more dramatic around the next bend to quash my disappointment.

Neuro dove into the woods, emerged into a clearing, and approached a precariously long narrow bridge. As we shot under its metal arches, the ocean sparkled between its metal girders.

Peekaboo. Where's my ocean? There's my ocean. Despite its massive breadth and proximity, the dense forest often obscured the Pacific.

The bridge structure intercepted the sun, causing it to strobe, hypnotizing me until the sound of a lumbering Kenworth scared the octane out of me. Muster stations! Full alert! Killer incoming! An eighteen-wheel highway hog. A NimRod killer. These are the times you wish you were a special forces operative with a license to mount a Howitzer on your bars.

Bridges can be ambush traps. Like being lured into a box canyon. All means of escape blocked. No retreat. Death bears down. You cannot swerve far. The semi's tires launched a shower of road debris. Screeching, hissing, yelling, panting, until, at last, the beast slunk into its lane, gained the bridge, and disengaged. Was it a bloodthirsty appetite or a mischievous game of chicken, one the trucker would never lose?

Motorcycle Riding Rule #1: Everyone is Trying to Kill You!

It's a massive relief when they choose not to. But here's always another two-wheeler down the road The Kenworth approached, encroaching into my lane. I thought about raising the biker salute. Thanks for scaring the additives out of me, asshole! A professional driver wouldn't have done that. Only someone contemplating murder.

Over her enormous bosom, the heavy-set, dark-skinned lady in the cab leered down. Next time you're toast, biker-idiot! I started to raise my arm, but it's a dicey move, provoking a volatile semi. They share targeting information by radio.

The tinted visor concealed my face, so the trucker couldn't see my credentials. Did she profile all motorcyclists the same way? You're all alike and way too free. Equal targets. Annoying, senseless creations. Not hauling freight. No waybills. Just bugs in my way. I will destroy your puny machines at a time and place of my choosing!

It is the power of eighteen wheels—to crush and destroy.

Motorcycles never attack.

Enormous Bosom Lady smiled and nodded. Sorry! Allow me to rub your helmet between my very large breasts.

I glanced back at the massive bully and read: This Truck Stops at All Railway Crossings.

Lordy. Lordy. Afraid of trains are you?

Eighteen-wheel weenie!

My Motorcycle State of Mind? A Bit of a Train Wreck.

* * *

Be Prepared to Stop

Followed by a long line of orange cones. We mean business! Absolutely no farting around, the signs implied! Four more signs. Twenty cones. Then a machine with one of those triangle warning symbols. From the shoulder, a mower on a long arm stretched out to cut grass and saplings, making it impossible for kamikaze deer to crouch low, out of sight.

I applauded the mower and rolled by the spectacle without incident. Keep up the good work! My reward? Another sign:

Resume Speed

Thanks! Neuro complied. Further along, I noticed a hole in the road. A colossal scar about the size of my top case. A crater capable of distorting wheel rims, throwing riders headlong into the mournful stillness. Wailing ambulances arrive, but it's too late. "Another Blockhead rider! Drove right into the hole. We wouldn't have been called out, had it been a car."

On either side of the hole, not a leaf stirred. Animal shapes crouched in the forest, peering out toward the chasm. They waited for Neuro to hit the hole and fling fresh meat over the bars. Human roadkill for ravens, coyotes, and maggots. But I was using my noggin to keep the rubber side down.

What to do—ignore the hazard, or swing around and implore the crew to act? They could at least put up one of their **Motorcycles Use Extreme Caution** signs. But highway workers honor a long-standing tradition—channel all requests through Planning at Regional Office.

No way I was going to divert to Regional to file a TR-139A.

I considered undertaking a citizen repair. Without a checklist and equipment, I could only toss stones randomly into the hole for hours, if not days. Amateurs are sitting ducks without yellow vests, warning signs, orange cones, heavy equipment, and walkie-talkie-equipped flaggers. Filing a TR-139A made good sense.

"Whoever knows the right thing to do and fails to do it, for him it is a sin," the Good Book states. If a biker was crippled because of the neglected crater, I'd stand accused of not doing the right thing. The media would make a big stink about road safety, causing Regional to react and do the right thing. Possibly a better solution than attempting a citizen repair? Sacrifice one rider for the greater good.

Confident I had the right thing nailed, I approached with caution. Neuro easily skirted the hole. I looked down. It wasn't top case size after all. More of a depression, really. An illusion like craters on the moon.

They appear enormous from Earth. When Neil Armstrong touched down in one, he observed, "More of a depression, really."

I'd have had grease on my face if I'd submitted a TR-139A. "Amateurs," the staff would scoff. "Biker-idiots."

Craters got me thinking about raison d'être. Neil Armstrong found himself on the lunar surface because President John F. Kennedy planted a stake in the ground. "We choose to go to the moon. ... The most hazardous and dangerous and greatest adventure on which man has ever embarked," Mr. Kennedy said. The nation was proud, but going to the moon lacked staying power. Neil hopped around the crater, then thought, Now what? He was not inclined to stay on the moon forever—no restrooms or shrubs to hide behind. No one was thirsting to be the second person on the moon.

Mr. Kennedy also stated, "There are no new horizons." Good thing he wasn't addressing the Horizons Unlimited Motorcycle Club. If you have a motorcycle, reaching the moon is unnecessary. Motorcycles open the door to new horizons—it's what they do.

I had plenty of time, so again I tossed Marta's raison d'être speech into my I Don't Care bin. *Marta, no one needs a reason to go for a ride.*

Then I saw a squirrel loitering the way they do before they leap, bound, and prance. They are the happiest wild creatures on the planet. You never see squirrels sulking or reptiles snaking around full of squirrel-like jubilation. You may spot snakes grinning as they swallow squirrels alive. Snakes don't leap from the shadows to attack riders, but you better watch for the buggers when you step down.

The squirrel vanished into the undergrowth.

That's the thing with motorcycle travel: life continually appears and then vanishes.

15

Squirrels and Impermanence

Down a dizzying slope we flew, pulled by the power of gravity, the engine freed of its burden. We scampered across a straightaway like a bird carried on the wind into a clearing. Neuro may have spread a pair of wings and soared had we not encountered this sign:

SLOW TO 35 MPH

It also indicated the reason: a sharp curve to the right. Neuro slowed, but used discretion.

We rode into another tract of clear-cut forest. Wounded remains sprawled about like decapitated creatures. Rejected to rot. Not worthy of the harvest. A dull and oppressive scene, like discarded bike frames left to rust.

Out of this carnage came a squirrel. It leaped onto a decaying log, its tail signaling delight. Squirrels possess unbounded cheerfulness matched by a resolute heart and inexhaustible energy. Life implants a raison d'être in these little creatures at birth. There is no guesswork—get right to exploring for food. Gather, repeat, and forever love the hunt.

Squirrels are born to search for nuts, not the meaning of life.

Ride with vigor. Gather your acorns. Be joyous. *Marta—be more like a squirrel?*

My Motorcycle State of Mind: Squirrely.

Squirrels are sweet creatures because they have clear, peaceful marching orders. They have no doubts or unfulfilled ambitions. They are nice, but I wouldn't lose sleep if Neuro flattened one. Same goes for most people. I never cry about human tragedies unless there's a motorcycle involved. Is there something wrong with me? "So many people are nicer when they're dead," I heard a celebrity say. People in the limelight take flak for statements like that. The sanctioned view is "Everyone is valued."

Not really. Motorcycle Cunts—now there's a group needlessly taking up space. Why not wipe them out along with healthy cagers who park in handicap spots? Don't shed a tear. Squirrels remain on top of the world even when one of their own is flattened by an eighteen-wheeler.

I'll definitely cry when my dog Pearly dies. Losing a pet is like saying goodbye to a motorcycle; it leaves me with a deep emptiness. Makes for a tough week, until I'm able to look back and celebrate the miles ridden, trails walked, and look forward to the joy of a new pet or machine.

"Be More Like a Squirrel." I repeated as a test. *Marta, another revolvement: Be More Like a Squirrel.*

Squirrels were everywhere in the clearing, out in the open, because they have nothing to hide.

Neuro's suspension went up and down, cushioning rough pavement. I moved lazily, thinking of all kinds of distant things. I looked at my GPS and thought it must have stopped. What has become of time and distance?

I made a pledge: I will start carrying nuts for squirrels. Chipmunks included—unless you're a wildlife biologist, it's impossible to tell the difference.

My Motorcycle State of Mind? Snug in my Chamber of Imagination.

A few miles later, I no longer gave a nut about squirrels.

16

Astoria

We passed farmland cleared many decades ago by homesteaders. How they must have toiled. Now their abandoned buildings were piles of caved-in decay. The grass grew tall. Thickets took over hay fields. Rodents found shelter under collapsed timbers.

The mystery: what caused this home to be renounced? What led the homesteaders to proclaim: Land, you are not good for us! Not productive. Too far from town. Inhospitable. Infertile. You hide snakes in your grass. We bet you had merit, but you do not. For fifty-seven years our family struggled. Hoping, but always left hungry. Cold. Attacked by forces beyond our control. This is a place of wasted lives. Land, you are not good.

If only they had motorcycles to ride away.

Where is this family now?

The questions asked, Neuro and I drove on.

Who gives a shit?

I'd be more interested in learning the fate of my old bikes. Only fragments of the experiences we shared remain with me. Most of all, the mechanical problems I attempted to overcome with fix-er bikes. I remember the faint odor of each machine, the shade of their oil and the different ways each communicated with me. Why did I replace them, sometimes with less accommodating machines? Why didn't I keep the best ones and explore many more happy miles? Why was I always on the lookout for the latest model and innovation, subject to the opinions of marketeers and peers? I suppose it was Motorcycle Narcissism—look at me on my new machine! The excitement of fresh steel and paint soon wears thin and the hunt for the next beauty resumes. I owned many bikes over the years.

Now I own reliable and comfortable. "You're getting old," Earl says.

* * *

I stood alone in an Astoria motel parking lot in the morning air. Then Easy Rider emerges from room 138. He sauntered over to his chopper and started cleaning. Despite wearing regalia, he looked like Coach Marvin. "Good morning," Coach Marvin. I took Neuro's cover off. "Keeps the salty sea mist off," I said.

It's hard to cover a chopper. "Morning," Coach Marvin said. He threw up his right arm for a moment as though he were brandishing a weapon and then let his cleaning rag fall. "Have to wipe mine down." The chopper looked immaculate. I pictured Stu's friend Klaus on it singing, ♪I'm beginning to feel like a Half-Biker. Half-Biker◈.

I put the cover in my top box and my travel bag in the right-side case. There was a time I'd lug many belongings on and off. Each morning I'd marvel as my more methodical friends got organized. I'd dread the prospect of being the only one not ready at the designated kickstands-up time. Don't know why this doesn't fit today. Yesterday it was fine. Now I carry little and worry less. "It's nice that the motel provides cleaning rags."

"Yes," Coach Marvin agreed.

Motorcycles deliver us to people we would otherwise never meet. "That's why bikers have a broad perspective," Marta says.

Coach Marvin was christened Philip. I asked about the feather stuck on the bar and he said he was part Native American.

"Nice," I said, demonstrating my sensitivity.

"Arapaho. One-quarter."

A mix of genocidal colonizer, scalper, and First Nation victim in one body.

"Now a biker," Phil said. "With a feather. I have a dirt bike ... at home in Montana."

Not a Half-Biker. Admirable.

"Riding to see what will soon be on the earth no more," he said in a sad tone. "Things are changing so fast."

Are they ever. It makes me worry about motorcycle cultural assimilation. Are we doomed to become Freeway Riders, stripped of our heritage? The last twisty roads bulldozed and straightened. Barred from our traditional grounds by metal gates. Two wheels bogged down in Road Vomit. No loud pipes. Don't stand on pegs. No lane splitting. No bare heads. Our heritage taken from us. Forced to accept cager laws and ways. Our mobility and free spirit stolen without compensation. My head was spinning.

"I hear you," I said, wondering about riding with Phil to see "what will soon be gone forever."

Coach Marvin—Phil—glowered. It may have been the glint from his chopper mirror. "I'd like to visit Vancouver Island. The ancestral home of the Coast Salish people."

I offered to show him around if he came—before we slide into oblivion.

I wondered if wind therapy is possible riding a chopper? The altered design reduces the front wheel's capability, forcing riders to be vigilant.

My Motorcycle State of Mind: Chopped.

* * *

Before I pulled out of the parking lot, it came: a barrage, shelling me, descending from a secluded fortification; the sound of metal folding, tearing, scraping, crushing. The threatening sounds compelled me to duck and hide, but stationary on-motorcycle, when a deluge begins, you remain exposed.

That's one thing cars are better at: protection.

I swiveled but saw nothing. A woman's cry rose in the air as if struggling to outdo the bombardment. Others followed. The woman wailed. Seagulls circled.

It's unsettling. Sitting motionless and vulnerable, threatened by an intimidating, harsh, destructive noise, not knowing which way to turn. Potentially in the line of fire, about to become collateral damage.

Suddenly, Coach Marvin was in front of me. Phil stared down the street, stepped back, and gave me the thumbs up. A police car, siren blaring, passed. I waved and pulled out.

Escape! Leave danger in the rearview mirror for others to deal with. Machines behaving badly. A car accident. Thank god for Coach Marvin. He blew his whistle and away I went.

South.

Soon I was out of the city limits and the day's trip began.

Glory and grandeur welcomed me. Neuro plunged into the solitudes, overgrown with trees, very brown and green, the sun at times blocked by a threatening cloud. For miles and miles, the serenity continued unbroken. Then the smooth sound of tires on pavement changed to rushing river water. I imagined Lewis scanning for danger, shouting orders. Paddles slapping and pushing, others waiting for a signal from Clark. Phil's indigenous ancestors thinking, *It's only a few. How bad can it be?*

An elderly man and woman leaned against an aging wooden fence and looked wistful as I zoomed by. Their dog barked. I wondered if Phil would stop and chat; they seemed like the sort that would get along. The couple looked as if they'd lost something.

Then I saw a large sign:

Home Run Café. World's Best Apple Pie. Left, One Mile.

A shiver ran up my spine.

As a general rule, motorcyclists are fond of pie.

My Motorcycle State of Mind: Drooling.

17

Honest Pie

I wasn't sure I was ready to pull over.

It's the trouble with wind therapy—steel and gas feedback can be cold and hard. You start to believe you're cured, but then you smell cinnamon from a roadside diner, and suddenly you need more information.

They say their pie is famous. That's how they always start—the lies. The World's Tallest Spruce Tree.

The thing about pie is: it's comfort on a plate. It shouldn't be messed with—not when riders are looking for comfort.

Academics will tell you that the Metropolitan Museum of Art, the British Museum, Los Alamos National Laboratory, Broadway, and Albert Hall house the world's best things. I've been inside the Louvre. It's where they keep the Mona Lisa. Let me tell you, it's pretty underwhelming. Nothing at all like crossing paths with a fully restored Brough Superior or world's best pie.

Frankly, I'd rather go to any motorcycle showroom than pay to get into a gallery like the Guggenheim. Not that I'm anti-art; it's a value-for-money proposition. I invested in *Motorcycle On Velvet*—it hangs in our garage.

The HomeRun Café is undiscovered and unpretentious. You'll find motorcycles parked in its lot and artful pie inside the restaurant, a converted house. The name is odd. SandCastle or Surf's Up are appropriate for Oregon beach country. PieHole would also be suitable. HomeRun Café? It seemed lost, like naming a motorcycle Lily Blossom. A sweet, fulsome scent carried by the breeze made me think, home run, if it tastes near as good as it smells.

**Homemade HomeRun Pie. Best in the World.
Enter from the side.**

What methodology do you suppose was used to determine Best in the World? Marta would ask. *Put a slice in it! Marta.*

Honest pie. Not those fried jam pastry abortions cagers pick up at drive-thru windows.

Neuro parked beside a Triumph. A powerfully built man bit into an apple. Braeburn, I expect it was. Forgetting the apple, I said, "Nice bike. Which model?" It's one of my go-to conversation starters.

"Thunderbird Storm." I already knew it was Triumph's "when too much power is not enough" muscle cruiser. He swallowed and said "HI" the way Marta does—HI THERE! HOW THE HELL ARE YOU FRIEND? So good to meet you. MUST BE MY LUCKY DAY!

"Bored out 1700?"

He nodded. "You bet."

"Braeburn? ... The apple?" I couldn't resist. It's a shot in the dark when much of the peel is gone.

"Gala ... Name's Pete. Friends call me Bear. My ex called me Papa Bear ... now it's You Gigantic Lump of Bear Shit." His roar left no doubt he'd moved on.

Steer clear of domestic squabbles—excellent advice. Stick with oil, mechanical specs, route info, cops, pets, or road hazards. Weather's OK if it's relevant. I reached for my phone. With a name like Bear, he must like animals, I thought. "My dog, Pearl." It's a conversation redirect technique. Always follow with a question. "Is your tire a little low?"

Pete smiled and peeked at his tires. "Cute. Corgi?"

"Corgi-shepherd cross." I put my phone away. "We had a goldendoodle. The ex has her now." Pete shrugged. "Wore away at her, I suppose. Took six years. Went on the skids just after I got my first bike. Folks who don't ride get pissed about the stupidest things." The big man's belly laugh rang like Shrek's.

Your ex was a *NimRod*? "Braeburns are one of my faves." He tossed his Gala core into the tall grass. I spotted a bit of pale apple peel and reprimanded myself for guessing Braeburn. "Ever had a Jonamac?"

Pete nodded yes. "Crispins can't be beat. Coffee? I'm buying." So, into the HomeRun Café walked two strangers headed in opposite directions. United by apples and motorcycles. I wondered if art lovers waiting to enter the Hermitage shared a similar bond?

Bear was a novice, having ridden for only a few years. "A kayaking guy," he called himself, but he was inquisitive about all things motorcycle. Every Velcro strap on his jacket asked, What? Tell me more. He thirsted for the truth about motorcycles. Most people rarely look beyond the lip of the little bowl of their life. After studying the menu pictures longer than I'd looked at the Mona Lisa, I leaned toward the HomeRun Apple Betty. There was much debate about the virtues of each pie on the menu and a futile attempt to rank apples by type. In the end, we settled. "Gotta go with the HomeRun Apple Pie." Made with four varieties.

Bear's Motorcycle Story

"Did a lot of ocean kayaking," Pete said. "If I could paddle at fifty miles an hour, I might still be on the water." Top kayak speed? Six mph with a favorable current and wind. "Can't see much of the world on a kayak."

I nodded. "But kayaks never get speeding tickets."

"Leaks though."

"Icebergs? Great whites? Marooned?"

We yakked to distract ourselves while waiting in a booth for pie. "You can eat pie in a kayak," Pete said. "But not on a bike."

"Can't pull into the HomeRun Café on a kayak."

Pete was on his way home, near Seattle. "A few days away. Meant to be a minor diversion, but it's been a shambles." Bear's Shrek laugh filled the room. "Guess I should have gone kayaking."

The pie arrived with coffee. In unison, our forks dug in. *Sweet Moses. Good gravy! Perfect pie*! I pointed and beamed.

Bear nodded. Thank god for motorcycles! He swallowed, then sang: ♪It never rains in California. It pours, man, it pours⊘.*Don't Sit Under the Apple Tree would have been more appropriate.*

"I'd planned to join three riding buddies in Mariposa. No deadlines, project schedules, or critical paths. People expect I'm joking when I mention I'm a programmer for one of the big boys." I'd have guessed logger or WWE wrestler. "But I sit in a cubicle in Redmond, Washington, staring at a screen, daydreaming, and doing inconsequential stuff with ones and zeros."

"Don't we all?"

"And daydreaming about riding away on my Triumph." Ocean kayaking used to be Pete's passion. "I'd sit in my kayak going nowhere fast, like a turtle, swearing at the racket when a motorcycle roared down the highway. Then, a few years ago, a colleague offered his old Suzuki GS500. Fit me like a minibike and ran like a leaky boat. A starter, he called it … 'To see if riding's for you.'" A couple months later, Bear sold his kayak and bought the Triumph. "No time for both. May buy another kayak one of these days. Or get a different bike." The California trip was also about Tara. "She could be a life changer. Felt the same about my ex. Now she calls me Bearshit." He bellowed while balancing a large chunk of pie on his fork. "Tara rides."

Honest pie paired with motorcycle chatter following a great ride.

My Motorcycle State of Mind? In pie heaven.

In Mariposa, Bear would join Tara on an 850 GS and Brad on his 1200 GS, a bike better suited to Bear than Brad. "Tara and I aren't a thing, but I have a crush. She's not hitched to Brad." Anson would join the group from the Bay Area on his Yamaha FJR. He'd signed on with a Silicon Valley startup and was pestering Bear to jump ship. "Investor mixers aren't for me," Bear said. "Hard to beat the weather in California, Anson keeps telling me." Bear tapped his plate. "Could go for another slice."

I agreed.

"Why not a whole pie each?"

At 4 p.m., three nights before we met at the café, Bear had checked into the Klamath Falls Motel 6 in south central Oregon. He went dark at ten thirty. Inexpensive motels often require tolerance, so Bear dragged a pillow over his head. Two men spoke in loud, indignant voices outside the window.

"Fuck that! Fuck this! Like fuck I will!" Obnoxious drunks. Ten minutes passed with barely a pause; the men only grew louder. Pete got out of bed, went to the window in his underwear, and inched the curtain open. The men, about Bear's age, were smoking and talking construction. Both had ample bellies hanging over their belts.

"I'm generally easygoing, but when something needles me, it feels like ten thousand devils nudging me to kick ass." Bear yanked the curtain open and tapped on the glass. His head motioned. Move along!

The reply was immediate—a finger from one, then the other—"Fuck you, asshole! Hunk of shit! Mind your own goddamn business! Who the fuck do you think you are? Don't tell us what to do!" Not here. Not at the Motel 6. One man flicked the ash of his cigarette toward Storm as if to say, *This is where we make our stand. We're not taking any more bullshit.*

"Behaving like backfiring engines," the Tony's gang would have said.

The men knew nothing about Bear. They didn't know he was forty-two, the son of an Ethiopian mother and Dutch father. Twenty-three years ago, a strong man who left the family home near Chicago to play football for the NCAA Cougars in Pullman, Washington. "Would have cracked the Seahawks' lineup, but a shoulder injury took me out. Ended up with a computer science degree instead." Pete sighed; the big man possessed a logical, gentle mind and a powerful, professionally trained body designed to intimidate and crush. He needed sleep, but now this. Go through the motions. Pull pants on. Sandals. Let his physique take charge. His massive neck. Broad shoulders. Huge forearms. For good measure, the armored jacket went on. Coach revved him up—*Go get* 'em, Pete! Flatten those pricks! The door opened, and the ex-footballer took a long, quick step forward.

Startled, the men shuffled back. Another step forward.

Go get 'em, Pete! Take the pricks down!

The men backpedaled.

Bear glared like a beast cornering its meal.

"OK, man. We're going." The drunk furthest from Bear said, "Don't get your panties in a knot, King Kong," and flicked his cigarette butt toward Storm.

All at once, the son of a bitch was sinking with his mouth open and his eyes bugged out. Bear had driven his elbow into the man's solar plexus.

"Risky," Bear told me. "Big makes you a trophy. Never know who's carrying."

I nodded as if it were a shared concern.

"It's why kayaking is great. Wind therapy, sure, but bikes can also raise hell. Not much happens on the water."

I pointed to the pie. "See how things work out, Pete? You climb on and everything changes. Quickly."

Bear let loose with a Shrek laugh that rattled my bones. "Best pie of my life," he said.

* * *

The following morning, Bear had walked back from the motel office carrying a feeble cup of coffee. Instinctively and adoringly, his eyes went to Storm. "Son of a bitch!" Lukewarm liquid dribbled onto his hand. He set the cup on the asphalt and leaned to investigate. A puncture.

"Had a repair kit but never used it. Then I saw the tear in the sidewall, an unrepairable gash." Storm was a casualty of war. "Kayaks don't get flats. They sink."

Pete kicked the tire and threw the rest of the coffee on the ground. He went to his room and lay on the bed, waiting for calm. After a bad play, step back and refocus. Three motorcycle shops came up on his phone—there was hope in Klamath Falls. Pete sent Brad a text: "Flat. Need new tire. Won't make Mariposa before Sunday.[Frowning Face]"

A minute later, a reply came. "Bummer. Tara had a battery problem. Didn't make it. [Sad Face]"

A little after nine, the second shop, the one that listed motorcycle repair on their website, answered. The guy who picked up understood the desperate circumstances. He likely had a tire in stock that "will get you home."

Bear waited. A Metzler. Just one. Pricey, but cost doesn't matter when you're in dire straits. "Find its mate when you're home."

The mechanic turned up with his truck and tools, took the wheel off, hauled it back to the shop, mounted the tire, returned, and put the wheel back on. Bear didn't lift a finger.

"He looked exactly like Charles Bronson in The Mechanic." Of ordinary build, calm, with only a faint expression and a few soft words. "Figured he'd take up the hunt. Use his local knowledge to track the drunks down and demand justice! Instead, he told me to get on with my trip. Best to forget about it." Bear shook his head. "Ain't worth stewing about," the mechanic said.

Bear booked a second night at the Motel 6.

He left the curtain open, but justice was denied.

Life is not always fair.

* * *

Storm turned out of the parking lot and headed for the border and "soon my mind flipped from zero to one." South on CA-139 under an overcast sky, toward Susanville for lunch. "Like picking up a fumble and doing my bulldozer run."

"Something about riding across a border always invigorates me."

The bike had swayed, wearing off new rubber chicken strips. Pete sang: ♪It never rains in California♦. Factually, 17.3 annual inches of rain falls in Susanville, about half of Redmond's slow drizzle and seven times less than Queets, Washington. Gloomy Seattle isn't even in the top thirty wettest American cities. New Orleans, 63 inches. Boston, 44 inches. Across the pond, London, England, receives 25 inches. South Pole precipitation converted to rainfall, 0.091 inches. Cold, but a dry cold; makes a colossal difference, prairie folks swear.

South of Susanville, the sky became sinister. Mother Nature had bad intentions. Bear pulled over and put his kayaking jacket and rain pants on. An untested defense. At two o'clock, he was twenty-five miles north of Quincy, an area that receives over 30 inches of annual rainfall, one of the wettest spots in California.

"It didn't look good."

"You were in California," I said. "How bad can it get?" I'd spun the Motorcycle Roulette weather wheel and lost more times than I care to remember. These days, I play it safe. I'd have sat tight in Quincy. Why gamble on the two-hour run to Lake Tahoe turning into hours of Motorcycle Misery? But he spun the wheel. I watched Bear scrape the last pie crumbs from his plate. He's not a person of half measures, I thought.

"When it started, it was like clean oil dripping from a bad gasket. Thick rain … saturated everything." The Triumph moved by motels on the north end of town. "I hate ending short of my planned destination, which was west of Tahoe. Play hard. Own the end zone."

Not a Half-Biker? Stubbornness often clobbers riders.

"Trained into me. A thousand daggers pushing me on." Reluctantly, Pete had geared down to check the last motel on the east side of town. The motel sign wasn't on. A solitary car sat in the lot. Closed, the sign said. "An omen, I figured. Never surrender, not one yard! Always down the field!"

I nodded. "So, despite a worsening downpour and knowing it was stupid, you were compelled to drive on?"

"Exactly."

I've been there. The Tony's gang calls it, "Forward the Light Brigade!" It'll be fine. Charge for the guns!

"Figured there'd be a place on the back road long before Tahoe. Away I went." The elevation increased as Storm traveled deeper into the Sierra Nevadas, and the temperature had plunged. "Felt like I'd ridden into a scene from The Outer Limits. Thick, violent rain, smashing into the pavement and bouncing back up. And freezing fucking cold."

It was one of those situations where the laws of common sense are defied. Logically speed should decrease, but the Triumph revved higher. Pete had implemented the get-there-as-soon-as-possible tactic. I've employed it many times.

"Between the rain and the condensation, I was practically riding blind. Kayak rainwear sucks on a motorcycle. Not made to handle the wind. Wasn't long before my body was numb." The cager in Bear spit and cursed at him: Cars provide shelter. They come equipped with heaters and wipers. What the fuck's wrong with you, biker-idiot? On-motorcycle, you must surrender to Mother Nature. She can toss you around at will, like a log on the ocean. Doesn't matter if you're Bear-sized. All you can do is tell yourself, This road has an end. Hold on and grind it out. "I was vibrating like a shaker basket."

Welcome to Motorcycle Misery, Bear! Far worse than kayaking; drowning is quick and peaceful. I wanted to laugh, but for the rookie's sake I didn't. The memory wasn't far down the road. It would be insensitive.

"No motels or roadhouses, just more horrible weather. I've never been so miserable. Thank Christ I had my ten thousand devils pushing me: keep going, you son of a bitch! I really wanted to curl up beside the road."

As Pete talked, I thought of Ernest Shackleton's team dragging their sleds across Antarctic ice. They were as close to the end as determined people can be and still function. The Sierra Nevadas can feel like Antarctica. Add in motorcycle wind chill and you may as well be pulling toward the pole.

"I almost caved, but Storm never stumbled."

Bikes can show persistence. I remember my bikes whispering, come on, just a little further. Hang on, we'll make it. Motorcycles always believe they can reach the South Pole.

* * *

Bear had stomped about, clapping his hands like an out-of-whack piston. Rapid breathing. Pale skin. Dripping wet. Shoppers in the Tahoe strip mall shook their heads. Who's the NimRod now, tough guy?

"Rolled out of my kayak once. Four degrees above freezing. Wasn't as bad." Pete peeled his gloves off, then headed to the coffee shop, trying to look normal. He didn't.

I know that feeling. Motorcycles can drain you.

"Could barely speak when I ordered. Squeezed the mug hard to transfer heat."

A text from Anson: "can't make the trip. Work. You know what it's like being the new guy. Enjoy. [smiley face]"

Bear messaged back: "Heading home tomorrow. [tire emoji]"

"When I finally checked in, the clerk said I looked bedraggled, polite, for you look like shit."

* * *

"Woke up to a California poster day yesterday," Bear told me.

"Blue skies to wipe bad memories away."

"Used the hair dryer to dry my gear and was glad to be heading home."

He headed west toward I-5, away from the foothills, grind it out in sparse traffic country. Pete cranked the throttle to slightly below *Born to Be Wild*.

Soon, a cop waved Storm over.

Bear switched the engine off. The cop made him sit and wait before asking, "Know how fast you were going, sir?"

Bear shook his head. *Did you hear about the incident at the Klamath Falls Motel 6 the night before last? Any leads?*

"Eleven over."

Pretty good, Bear thought. "Would have guessed more." Why did you stop me? The officer rattled on. It seemed to Bear that if he had poked his forefinger through the protective regulation vest, he'd have found nothing inside but a one-size-fits-all rule book. No fair play or live-and-let-live leeway. No audibles.

"Could have mentioned my Seahawk days. Lots of cops are football fanatics."

Bear plunked the ticket down on the table. "Three hundred and forty-seven bucks."

"Gave you a break, sir," the cop had said. "Could have been four sixty."

How about subtracting the crime spree?

"Drive safe, sir," the trooper had said, satisfied he'd prevented another motorcycle mishap.

"Right," Bear answered and screamed at the last couple of days. You can do that on-motorcycle.

"Kayakers never get speeding tickets," I said.

The HomeRun Café filled with Shrek laughter.

* * *

Outside, Bear said, "It's weird how, once a shitty road trip is barely in the rear-view mirror, it toughens you. Makes you giggle. Bad kayaking stories just remain bad memories."

"Life changes quickly on-motorcycle. Maybe that's why the worst trips soon make the best stories?"

Bear nodded. "Takes a long time to build distance paddling a kayak. Things change slowly. Just more water."

Like a couple of giggling adolescents, we swapped contact info and vowed to meet again. Saying "till next time." It felt like a huggable moment.

We didn't.

When Bear left, he honked.

I gave him a thumbs-up and pulled out. The crust of the pavement was crumbly near the shoulder. Centerline held firm like a well-baked apple pie.

18

Coffee Stops

The motel ceiling stared back like it was waiting for an update. The low-frequency hum of an AC unit droned on. Outside, a car idled, its engine committed to some direction. I drew the curtain—the sky was that bright but indecisive kind of blue, like it hadn't yet decided whether to bless or punish.

When I stepped out, the morning sun winked—*Good morning, friend! Mother loves you. Isn't it great to be alive, traveler?* I dawdled beside Neuro while the sun's rays embraced me.

"Be even better once I find decent coffee."

It was 7:30 a.m. when I left my room on foot, bound for the Coastal Bean a block away.

"Never ride without coffee." Earl means it.

"Earl, it's okay to ride a short distance to get good coffee." Then I explain it's not an absolute like Thou Shall Not Kill, it's just a cup of coffee. "If a cager were to run you off the road and then come at you with a knife, hollerin' and all jacked up, what you gonna do? Use common sense. Kill or be killed. Even the Commandments can be bent, so surely you can wait for your cup of coffee."

"Could be a Motorcycle Cunt coming at you ... jumped off a nice bike to kill you," Earl had answered.

"Sure." I nodded, playing along. "Could happen."

"I'd go for the eyes."

"Genitals."

"Throat."

"Or turn the other cheek?"

We both laughed.

"Suppose," Earl said, "you're riding a fixer and the Cunt you killed had your dream bike. Do you take it?"

That's a tough one. "Break two rules in one day? Many scholars say Thou Shall Not Steal refers to stealing a human being."

"Kidnapping."

"So, taking the nice bike would be the sensible thing to do."

Thanks to being solo, my walk to the Coastal Bean wasn't up for debate. In a group, there would have been a compulsory review. But being solo has a shadow side. After a couple of good days, you get cocky. Everything is going well. It's easy to think you're fine on your own, but then the weather turns. Your bike runs rough. The next curve tries to throw you.

Sitting with your riding buddy is the cure—warm and reassuring, like a cup of coffee.

My Motorcycle State of Mind: In need of coffee.

For me, bold roast at a local shop is part of the ritual. Sip and plan my day. Then drive, searching for cup two. More pleasure awaits down the road.

At the Bean, I started a text. "Bear, when you turned west from Tahoe, did you realize you were a wheelie or two from the Donner Pass?" Bear would be busy with home base stuff, so I tapped Delete. Bear's Sierra Nevada misery tale pales compared to the Donner story.

November, 1846, weather trapped eighty-one souls. Forty-five members of the party survived the winter, allegedly by turning to cannibalism. It was Before Motorcycle. Still, the worst trips make the best stories.

"Trust you're home safe and sound, Pete. Maybe Beartooth Pass this summer?"

Before my cup was empty, a reply came. "Beartooth for sure! And pie. Ride safe!"

As I left, I passed a cager hunched over a giant pastry like it was his final meal.

***

In the lot, I looked Neuro over. Holy Toledo! That magnificent creature is with me! A tingle ran up my spine. I wish I could show you her photo, but I swore to be machine incognito.

There my partner stood, waiting for me.

My Motorcycle State of Mind? Blessed.

Per standard practice, I'd gassed up the previous night. "I'm ready," Neuro called. "Hop on. Let's go!"

Following a few quick wipes and checks, we were under way, proud and free. The sun paused behind a cloud, making for a soothing grey contrast, damping the glare of the morning light. I looked at a black-and-white landscape. Then the sun's rays colored it in.

Relaxed, I looked forward to cup two at a local shop. ♪One more cup of coffee for the road◊. The sun laughed. A car passed. The driver had takeout coffee and a fried pie. Probably tuned into fake news. It's a combination that clogs brains. The driver appeared to be annoyed.

"Don't wait for National Relaxation Day," I shouted. That's August 15th.

"Should be called NimRod Bug Out Day," Den says.

I loosened my grip, rolled my shoulders, stretched each limb, and drew a deep breath. Neuro purred. We were easygoing and going easy. Letting it roll down the highway.

"Be more like squirrels!"

Riding under broken clouds beside a heavy sea can make every pulse and artery of my body swell and burst with appreciation.

Then I leaned forward to scrape my pegs.

Using good judgement, I twisted the throttle. Here's my thinking: to recondition a brain you must move beyond the bell curve, on both ends. The hunt for cup two was on. ♪One more cup of coffee for the road◊.

***

Highway 101 changes as you drive south. The further you go, the more the institutionalized anti-motorcycle sentiment of the people-in-charge becomes apparent. The Oregon Coast is especially hostile in July and August. Unless you can tolerate congestion, stay away. Road Vomit will trigger Falling Down rage. It is a time when RVs creep. Parades hem bikes in. Cops wait to pounce. It's a pig's breakfast of cager tourism.

Mid-June, with unseasonably cool temperatures, it was perfect. Thank you, Mother Nature, for being a sweetie and keeping the Nim-Rods on home plate!

Three hundred and sixty miles of magnificent coastline to explore. Massive cliffs. Beaches with rocky sands and large, unique stack formations to marvel at from a front row seat on-motorcycle. White waves that pound into dark rocks. Neuro would pass the largest expanse of oceanfront sand dunes in the USA. Dunes towering up to 500 feet. Best of all, there are stretches of the old highway that have eluded modernization.

I rode headlong into whatever came my way, diving, bending, jumping, snaking, slowing. Neuro clattered over a deserted rail crossing, rumbled through a sleepy village, and then charged through a series of curves beneath a threatening sky. The lumbering ocean mist retreated. The sun broke through. I switched Neuro to Cruise Mode. Relax. Let's run below the bottom end of the bell curve for a bit.

The rhythm of my heart was in synch with the engine—calm, steady, in harmony with the machine. There can be contentment in plodding. "Life is not a race, it's a journey," a wise person said.

Until you're presented with beautiful curvature. There was no holding Neuro back. She sped out of the first bend and continued through another to a sign that read:

SLOW TO 45 MPH

I gave it the biker salute. Life is complex. Despite the good intentions of lawmakers, it cannot be reduced to a single speed.

The fourth curve rattled me. I gritted my teeth so my heart couldn't speak of my unpardonable sin, having a machine under my care and not being exact. Too much oil. Not enough air. Too little awareness. At the apex, loose gravel threatened Neuro. I panic-braked when I should have been smooth. You think you know it all and are rock solid, but that's not how it works. Shit can happen out of the blue, knock you silly, kicking experience and skill to the curb. Each curve is like a moon shot—miscalculate, and you're in deep space. I must make better use of my noggin. Or observe cager speed limit signs.

I slowed, breathed, and coasted. A SQUID Blockhead would have been in the weeds. Instead of a swift kick in the sensors, I applauded myself.

My Motorcycle State of Mind: Survivor.

I'm timid of deer, not bends in the road.

A wall of water on one side. On the other, a continent reverberating with the hollow, ponderous beats of humanity. Neuro pulled up a long hill and past a truck lugging, needing to gear down, suffocating on its exhaust. Panic-braking in a semi would be peculiar. Big rigs run up hills and then place all their faith in the physics of resistance. Truck drivers gear down, fearing a suicidal pace should their brakes fail. On the worst hills, there are runaway lanes. Conrad watched a truck rocket up one once, on the verge of total catastrophe, revving high, mud and water flying, the driver hollering, "Gravity, gravity, where art thou gravity? Save me!"

"Suddenly it was all right," Conrad said. "By some Newtonian law, machine and driver saved."

Conrad's lucky. I don't know anyone else who's seen a runaway semi.

I glanced in the mirror at the truck behind me. It was coughing, but it persisted. At the crest of the next hill, I turned into a viewpoint. Why not? Unlike the truck driver, I wasn't on a schedule. I checked my phone: a Marta text. "Any good stake-in-the-ground ideas?"

I swiped IGNORE. *Marta, I Don't Care!*

As I was about to climb back on, a couple pulled in, so I paused. The man and woman marched toward me like we were old pals. It was

odd because I'm used to Marta or Conrad being the greeter and stranger magnet, in charge of preliminaries. Being socially lazy, I come in off the bench and offer a few grunts. Chatting is in my friends' DNA. Both Marta and Conrad have long conversation attention spans. I have to pry them away. Did we come to visit or to ride? Solo, the calls are all mine. Had enough? Walk away. Unless you're working on your mindset, in which case it's best to be sociable. Allow yourself to be reconditioned.
I checked their motorcycle plates. Good gravy! A long way from home. "Hello, friends!"

19

Balance, Brakes, and Beliefs

The lone rider image is that of a mobile, antisocial hermit, a North Korean renegade. God knows what misery awaits this unattached misfit down the road. By the grace of God, one day he'll find peace, buy a car, and settle down.

"You'd be surprised," I replied.

"Very surprised," Dori said.

I didn't drone on about biker camaraderie, the bonding MAGIC of the machines, or the embrace of wind therapy. Solo is a portrait of solitude—a single bike on Desolation Road. A long, long way from home. "Trust me. It's not what it seems." I smiled.

Dori nodded sarcastically. "Sure."

Tony's right: "You've got to polka if you want to party."

I wore no off-putting regalia, the kind that shouts: stay the hell away! I'm a lone wolf, possibly a maniac. No skulls, crossbones, bizarre tattoos, or swastikas. I wasn't wrapped in a hi-vis yellow reflective material, buzzing in a swarm of lookalike bees. Run away or we'll sting! No, I wore a grey jacket. A neutral color. The color of gravel and granite. Solid as a rock, it says. Come on over and chat, friends. I'm safe and neutral like Switzerland. Perhaps a wee bit bland.

There's another school of thought amongst those who study how colors affect human physiological processes—grey is the color of mental confusion. It's halfway between opposites, white and black. Say the wrong thing and people swear, This jackass is one of those gray over grey types with an out-of-whack state of mind. Devoid of long-term goals.

Unable to settle on color or color. That sort of thing. You never see grey motorbikes, but it is a very popular automobile choice.

At the viewpoint, I took my jacket off.

I enjoy being Switzerland, letting Marta, Conrad, or whomever pontificate. I'm happy to skip chairing committee meetings, wear my frown upside down, and not adopt a stated position. Making contact is in my friends' wheelhouses. I need reminders. Don't slouch! Pay attention! Answer the question! Raise your hand. Don't walk away. Smile! Don't fold your arms. Look people in the eye. Don't come across like a curmudgeon! Receptive cues like those. I must remind myself of Tony's advice: "Just polka."

If I reach down, I can pull sociable off. "Hello there, where you headed on your motorcycle?" strangers ask. Are you Swiss, by any chance?

"Down the coast" doesn't impress, so I tag on something like, "A few years ago I rode to Tapachula." Or "I may explore the remotest region of Mongolia next year." Perhaps I'll sign onto the Electric Bike on Mars project.

"Really?" Strangers have no concerns about solo explorers wearing plain grey jackets as long as the welcome flag is flying.

"Is it okay to take a picture of Sally and Johnny in front of your motorcycle, mister?" I had that happen once; I was wearing my pale green jacket.

"Cagers on road trips are interesting creatures," Marta believes.

"Out of their cars, they're less likely to kill you," Conrad always adds.

Travelers are a community. Like off-leash dogs—it's natural to sniff out different breeds. Just avoid being a pit bull with a spike collar and a muzzle.

Parked at the viewpoint, I wasn't surprised when the Saskatchewan couple, who arrived on separate bikes, approached me. I was holding my grey jacket[,] so my Tony's tee shirt was front and center.

My Motorcycle State of Mind: Let's Polka!

***

I could tell they were shaky when we said hello.

"BC?" the woman asked.

"Victoria."

"It's the war," Black Jacket with White Reflective Strips (Clay) said.

"Seems you can't escape," Green Touring Jacket added.

"Even in Texas, war broke out. What the hell is wrong with our world?"

I suppose, standing proud alongside Neuro, I looked like the sort of person who had answers. "There's a war in Texas, you say?"

Green Touring Jacket, (Donna), nodded. "Attacked by motorcycles."

Generals agree: motorbikes are poor annihilators. They're best used to avoid conflict. I was leaning on Neuro so couldn't deploy the "got to get something from my bike" excuse to walk away.

"War can pop up anywhere," Black Jacket with White Reflective Strips, "Clay," said.

"Even on a highway in Texas."

What are you whack-a-doodles talking about? I put my jacket back on, prepared to use the always reliable, gotta hit the washroom excuse.

Eventually, I realized they were pissed because of a Texan road rage incident, but more so because Vladimir Putin was "de-Nazifying Ukraine."

"The list of despots waging war goes way back," I said. "Not surprising." Long Before Motorcycle, King Leonidas proclaimed, "The world will know that free men stood against a tyrant, that few stood against many, and before this battle is over, even a god-king can bleed." Or was it Gerard Butler who portrayed Leonidas in the movie? In any case, the Persians really did kick the shit out of the Spartans in 480 BC. The king made an impassioned speech the world took no notice. Speeches, the United Nations, the threat of nuclear war, songs like *We Are the World*, not even motorcycles can stop us from waging war.

"Just ride," Marta says. "Guard your individual balance. Forget about saving humankind."

"Putin should bleed," the couple said.

I profiled the Russian dictator as Grendel, the creature of darkness from the epic poem Beowulf. Exiled from happiness and accursed of God.

Green jacket, Donna shrugged. "I don't understand why these assholes are never taken out. Instead of bleeding, they live the high life."

Detente doesn't work. The UN's a wet noodle. Politics isn't a science. Need more? Mechanically, I pulled a glove on just as Clay said, "A couple of grade A, no preservatives added, completely natural pricks on motorcycles. In Texas."

I put the other glove down. *Tell me more.*

Donna and Clay's Motorcycle Story

"We needed a break. You know … a stick-your-head-in-the-wind break. Plus, it was Donna's birthday," Clay said.

"Who knew we'd be trapped in a war zone?"

They had flown to Dallas–Fort Worth International Airport. It was mid-April. "Rented a Japanese cruiser—seemed inappropriate, but the Star Venture was the best price. And anything with two wheels capable of two-up would do. We just wanted to cruise… in peace."

Clay rattled off their route. 35W, 67, 4, 1217 … Brains able to retain highway numbers annoy mine. Back roads, Dallas to San Antonio would have sufficed.

"The Star Venture spit out miles like a D9 Caterpillar, chewing up a golf path, revving low and turning easy." One hundred thirteen cubic inches wrapped in Raven Metallic Black. "Plowin' air," Clay called it.

He had turned forty-six, young enough to defend Ukraine's sovereignty. "Felt guilty not being in the fight. We both have relatives in the old country." In many armies, forty is too old to enlist in active duty, but not when Grendel's trampling on your border.

They had pulled over in Santa Anna to stretch. When they left for San Antonio, Donna was in command, her first stint driving a brute.

Two nights on the canal by the Alamo, sightseeing, strolling, relaxing. Birthday cake and beer. Short rides to the missions at the national park. A recipe for JOY.

Clay leaned against the backrest. "Being a passenger makes me uneasy, even on straight and flat. But we were there to forget shit, so I tried not to be a backseat Nervous Ned."

Donna nudged her partner.

"I trust this one," Clay said, "but prefer to be in the driver's seat."

"The Venture felt like moving from a pickup to a semi." Donna drove a well-used Can-Am 250 at home. Interstates aren't for dirt bikes. They're for Star Ventures, Harleys, Wings, choppers, and baggers. "Once I got the thousand pounds rolling, it was fine. Accelerating onto the highway was exhilarating." Donna's hand cut through the air.

"I bet." Right hand on the throttle, you pivot left to survey the river of cars. Maybe you push the turn signal button, but either way[,] you lean toward traffic, pick your opening, adjust speed, and point to the open slot. In you go to claim your space, careening along between five-thousand-pound killers. Hundreds of tires. The roar of exhausts. A rampage of cages. You try to fit in and adjust to a world where you are an outsider.

"Starts and stops were nerve-wracking," Donna said. "But driving the Venture on the highway was a breeze."

"Sure." Freeways are easy to take for granted, but can be unforgiving. In the world of cars and big rigs, motorcycles travel unseen, insignificant where mass is king. Seams and cracks in the asphalt are trivial to fat tires[,] but can take riders down. Debris can become a road mine. The wind from howling eighteen-wheelers can slap you silly. Eventually, the deluge settles into a dull roar and you struggle to remain observant.

Donna kept the Venture at the speed limit, slower than the vehicles needing to be somewhere. "Lumbering speed," she called it.

"Plowin' air," Clay, the schoolteacher, said. He believed in gradual immersion. "Take your time, ease in." He was well acquainted with fast, but it is slow that calms passenger uneasiness. Besides motorcycles, Superstock was Clay's passion. He had raced on tracks all over the Midwest, on both sides of the border. "Being a passenger sucks," he texted his pit guy, Bernie. "Next trip, two bikes."

Donna guided them down the highway through wide-open spaces. The sun beat on the monotone landscape. She tapped the side of her helmet and said, "Remember the Alamo." It had been their signature phrase since settling on Texas. The Tail of the Dragon and the Blue Ridge Parkway next year.

Clay pressed the intercom button. ♪Davy, Davy Crockett, King of the Wild Frontier◇. Donna pictured Ukrainian sunflowers flourishing in the peaceful Texan soil.

She slowed to duet. ♪Davy, Davy Crockett, King of the Wild Frontier◇.

"There was a noise, a great big hullabaloo … like a column of tanks." The couple stopped singing. Birds caught updrafts. Sunflowers sagged. Serpents slithered into holes.

"Let them go by," Clay said, his passenger anxiety surging.

"Everyone does." The Venture held slow and steady as the lead bike went by, a chopped Victory. The rider wore a leather vest with symbolic messages, chaps, and a skullcap with fiendish miniature horns. A witchman, the type that doesn't shop for grey, green, hi-vis, or plain leather. He wanted the Motorcycle Cunt look.

The second bike, a lightly modified Indian, drew even with Donna. The rider wore a vest with blue jeans and no helmet. Both men were older than Clay, well beyond the age when people say you should know better. They had long beards. Patches on their backs indicated a territorial or brotherhood claim. Stereotypes, Clay guessed. Probably city workers. They looked like powerful men gone to seed.

"ZZ Top?" Clay asked over the intercom.

"Sharp dressed men?"

"Cheap sunglasses?"

"Beautiful custom paint job ... on the Indian. A work of art." Clay wanted a FTR, the flat track model. He motioned, Go by. Instead, the Indian swayed toward the Star Venture.

Donna swerved, wobbled, and then hugged the outside edge of her lane.

"It's OK." But it wasn't, because the Indian veered toward them again.

A transport truck forced the Indian into its lane behind the Victory. The Motorcycle Grendels slowed to match Donna's pace. Then they slowed a little more. Donna braked. "Should I pull over?" she asked, shouting over the pipes.

"It's fine. Just horsing around," Clay answered, a helpless ornament stuck on the bench. "Bluffing, like schoolyard bullies." Picking on Japanese cruisers. Clay knew the type. Motorcycle racists.

"The chopper wouldn't be a problem," Clay told me. "A showpiece, not a road racer. Riding two-up on a straightaway, we'd be at a disadvantage against the Indian." But Clay had Superstock experience. On asphalt, he was king, but as pillion baggage, he was dead weight.

Ignore? Do nothing? Ride it out? I can deal with this, Donna had told herself. Just boys fooling around.

But when the powers of darkness assault, there's no knowing where the evil will land.

The Cunts rode side by side, forming a rolling barricade. Like Grendel Putin, they intended to subjugate.

A series of cars overtook the three slow-moving machines. The outlaws varied their speed and moved as necessary to block the Venture.

"I'm going to pull over! This is insane."

"Wait till we see a car. There'll be one soon. Push back as soon as I'm off."

Donna held at thirty in a sixty-speed zone. The Victory moved out into the left lane and then dropped back until it was parallel with the Star Venture. The rider scowled and stroked his groin. His bike revved, firing engine blasts, pressed into battle.

Clay pointed his cell phone; video, but no bars on his tourist plan.

The man on the Victory pointed his hand and finger like a pistol.

Donna slowed to twenty-five.

The man on the Indian in front of the Venture raised a handgun. The weapon swung in small circles.

Clay moved his phone from the Victory to the Indian. "It was surreal."

"Almost pissed my pants."

"We weren't sitting ducks," Clay said. "What with shooting backward from a moving motorcycle."

"Still, we could have been gunned down on a Texas highway. Like in a B movie."

"For renting the wrong bike and looking like tourists."

He holstered the gun. The chopper pulled forward, still in the wrong lane.

Clay returned his phone to his pocket.

A pickup approached, traveling fast.

The Venture slowed. The distance between it and the outlaws grew.

"The horn on that bike was so pathetic," Clay said. "I wanted to laugh."

The kickstand went down—a skill worked out at a Dallas Walmart. Clay was off. Donna pushed back. Well-oiled until Clay tried to swing his leg up over the seat. He wasn't used to a passenger blocking his movement.

"I had to slow down. Lose seconds. Climb on in a methodical, mechanical way. It's hard to do when you're revved up."

The pickup went by and the Venture fired up. "I was back on the track," Clay said. "In control. Challenging for the lead. I ran forward, toward the two bikes, until I found the second gear sweet spot."

The Indian had stopped in the middle of the highway. The driver was off, swinging his gun above his head.

"As we bore down on him," Clay said, "I thought of the grizzly. A few years back, I came up suddenly on it in the Rockies. I was on my

Ducati. It was the same feeling back then. At first, stunned ... then a shot of adrenalin made my heart race. Breathing sped up. Vision narrowed. I've always wondered what the bear was thinking as I bore down. Fight, flee, or freeze? Luckily, it went one way, I the other."

"The Grizzly didn't have a gun," Donna said.

Clay had pulled wide, leaned, and swung the big bike into a sharp turn.

"The Venture didn't falter. We made the change, straightened up, and were gone. End of story."

"So much for the brotherhood, sisterhood of motorcyclists."

"Machine racists," Clay said. "Or just fooling around?"

"Jacked up on something?"

"What would their mothers say?" Donna asked.

I shrugged. It's a mystery how motorcycles affect riders in such different ways.

Back in Santa Anna, the couple had shown the video to the police.

The cops assured, "We'll stop them."

The Venture followed a trooper toward San Antonio. Clay drove.

Donna leaned into the wind and tapped her intercom button. "Remember the Alamo."

The Star Venture rolled along. Together they sang: ♪Wherever we go, we'll remember the Alamo♦.

"Sunflowers rose from the desert," Donna said.

"Even god-kings bleed," I said.

"In the wind," Clay said, "Your perspective quickly changes."

"I hope those two find what it is they're looking for."

* * *

"So tranquil here." Then came another question without an answer: "Why must there be war?"

I almost answered. Almost. But balance isn't found in answers—it's found in the time between reactions. That's something riding teaches. On a tight curve, there's a moment where you stop thinking and just feel the lean, the grip, the line. You're not forcing the world to make sense. You're moving with it. Balance.

It's not about right and left. Throttle and brake. Speed or cruise. Attention and surrender. War or peace. Motorcycles demand harmony, or they take blood. Never push against the ride, let it carry you.

I dangled my keychain. It's a nervous habit, Dori says.

I like the symbol. The chain swung like a hypnotist's watch. "Balance," I said.

I'm not a philosopher, just someone who carries a yin-yang keychain. "Balance," I repeated, "is what the symbol represents."

The keychain was a gift from Marta. She handed a slew of them out one Christmas. "Yin-yang and motorcycles are a perfect match," she declared at the time. "Both seek harmony in order to manage opposing forces. Motorcycles go down if the rider does not respect balance."

Thank you, Marta, I thought at the time, but I Don't Care!

"Motorcycles help with perspective. They are all about finding the sweet spot. Yin and yang." After a pause, I added, "The symbol's a great reminder."

It's impossible to talk yin-yang without coming across like a stripped bolt. Donna and Clay wanted real answers. When will Putin bleed? Why are there Motorcycle Cunts? Answers to questions like those. I responded by showing them a symbol, a keychain. "Everything is in motion, seeking harmony. There are motorcycle saints." I paused. "Peace follows war. Putin will bleed."

Donna nodded.

"Yin and yang."

Clay scratched his forehead. He was thinking exactly what I thought when Marta gifted me the keychain. What a steaming load of horse crap! I dangled the symbol and kept my mouth shut.

We absorbed the moment and then, as if adrift on the ocean, left in opposite directions. I heard Neuro whisper, Conrad's right. Best to keep the Motorcycle Yin-Yang thing between us. The engine revved and then slowed. Vehicles went north and south. The suspension traveled up and down. We leaned and counterbalanced. The tide went in and out. Trees grew and fell. Birds flew up and glided down. Day would turn to night.

I reported back to Marta: in my experience, Yin-Yang is amazingly reliable, except when humans are involved.

* * *

A few weeks later, I received a message from Donna and Clay. "Made it home safe and sound. No Cunts!" There was a picture of them each holding a Yin-Yang keychain. Not as nice as the ones Marta handed out, but close. "The ride goes on."

So it does.

The picture made me smile and then frown. Laugh and then pout. Reach out, but stop and think, I don't care.

Later, at home, I cleaned my keychain with a mild detergent before applying a dab of very expensive motorcycle miracle sealer. Grubby, then spotless, I thought.

20

Be Flexible or Stay Put!

I passed a column of waiters. At least ten vehicles had stopped in an unexpected area. Frustrated drivers gave me the look. *Wait your turn, biker-idiot! Back of the line!*

Behind a visor, it's easy to ignore standard protocols. Like the one they drill into elementary school kids. Single file. No butting in. Follow the leader. Wait your turn.

Whenever there's a snag, Earl repeats the same rule: "Be Flexible!" Just because they chose to drive cars doesn't mean we wait. Just because they painted a double line for cars.

I rolled like a rigid snake, slithering by the lineup. Had I strayed too far, oncoming traffic would have picked me off. It's always open season for queue jumpers.

At the head of the line, a large broken-down truck had its safety triangle out. Standing on the road was a young, overwhelmed driver. He intended to signal when it was safe for the waiting cars to go, but it never was. Meanwhile, the hornet's nest honked. Some began to seethe with rage. Others relaxed. A Grendel stroked his pistol.

Cars and trucks coming from the opposite direction slowed to view the situation but refused to yield their lane.

For the bewildered young truck driver turned traffic control director, I was the Light Brigade, charging into the gap, creating a distraction. Oncoming traffic slowed. The young man signaled halt.

Movement ceased, except for Neuro. We sped away. Be Flexible!

Thank you, Earl. Waiting in line is pure hell on a motorbike. Motorcycles must be in motion.

Motorcycles demand movement, but they also demand surrender. You can't force the weather to clear or traffic to part like the Red Sea. All you can do is adjust your line and stay upright.

I used to think being flexible meant speeding up. Now I think it means staying in the game. Not quitting when the road doesn't make sense. Maybe that's why Earl's rule matters.

***

The mist that ushered in the day had cleared, making the ocean visible for three miles. Somewhat less for those of us with presbyopia, but I was pleased to see about two miles of the Pacific. As I looked, I thought, Everything about this trip has been as smooth as silk.

I examined my state of mind and found it well-balanced. "Success," was my message to Marta, without an explanation.

I glanced at the yin-yang symbol. When extraordinary feels normal, it's time to shake things up. I was heading south, so I turned Neuro east. A great continent beckoned. Explorers of old were told, "Go west." Now, After Motorcycle, it was, "Go anywhere you damn well please." I nudged Neuro. There it is. East. Waiting for us. Let's have a peek, shall we?

GPS was pleased when I made its first stipulated turn. It had plotted a roundabout course on secondary roads—fifty miles to gain seven miles south.

Before electronic navigation, I'd have stopped and laid out crude charts on the ground. Used bits of string and then paused to make observations of paramount importance. My head would shake as I mulled over doubtful calculations. I know nothing about triangulation and little about dead reckoning.

Modern explorers are not navigators. We have no need to rely on the science as Ernest Shackleton did. Yet we travel hundreds of miles and arrive at our destinations within minutes of our GPS-predicted time. Donna confirmed in her text: home on time.

The gizmos are outstanding course-plotting, direction-finding wizards. My brain sometimes forgets where I parked the car, but my GPS knows the precise location of addresses and roads worldwide. It's mind boggling. Nevertheless, I often disagree with its thinking, even though it's akin to stepping into the theory of relativity ring with Einstein.

Despite being amazingly capable, the devices are vulnerable. GPS units are pigheaded. Einstein conceded that his Cosmological Constant Theory of a static and unchanging universe was flawed. Unlike Albert, global positioning systems never concede. They believe they always know what's best and refuse to budge. Their designers failed to impart what Albert recognized—the universe is continually accelerating and expanding. Like trail braking, string theory is impossible to comprehend.

I gave my GPS the benefit of the doubt and accepted its route as we strayed east. In parts, it was a maze, but the gizmo performed brilliantly. Then began the recalculations, but GPS always remained supremely confident. Just give me a sec. I'll have a new answer.

Neuro darted and dashed hither and yon—it was brilliant. No signs of civilization. The law of straight highways out the window. Away we went, more and more detached from the certainty of the coastal highway.

There are plenty of lost-in-the-wilderness stories. Slow death by GPS. Families left to freeze and starve because they failed to be Einsteins. They refused to accept the universe is constantly changing and went all in on a pigheaded device. My GPS had me on a questionable track.

Neuro coped well, but after one too many recalculations, I lowered the boom. GPS, you are sketchy! I seized control, pressed OFF, and swung Neuro around. I may not always find my car, but I have an intuitive sense of being off course. I let the smell of salt water be my guide.

Back on the highway, heading south, I pushed GPS ON. Widgets do not sulk, and my GPS got right down to business, resuming operations as if it had not been reprimanded. The exact opposite of humans. Imagine if Albert Einstein was navigating. There'd be bickering for miles. He wasn't quick to concede.

Neuro came up behind a fast-moving SUV. How do you overtake a speeding vehicle without speeding yourself? Albert would confirm it's impossible, but the louts-in-charge fail to comprehend. Automobile laws have subjugated motorcyclists. There are simple solutions. Like setting Motorcycle Speed Limits by following a MotoGP racer and rolling their top speeds back by a reasonable percentage. Instead, motorbikes are doomed to be outlaws. It's machine prejudice at its worst.

My Motorcycle State of Mind: Weighted down by the ugly reality of institutionalized discrimination.

Thank god for The Earl Rule! Be Flexible! I tore past the speeding SUV.

When I slowed to turn into Rockaway Beach, the SUV passed me.

I stopped at a Shell station knowing there was zero chance of meeting a motorcycle sage. They detest franchised operations. So, I visited the restroom without looking over my shoulder.

Oregon banned self-service for many years. In 2018, it was permitted in rural areas. For urban areas, lawmakers maintained this principle: Pumping gas is a hazardous activity best performed by properly trained professionals. Legislators cited seventeen reasons, including wet pavement leading to slips and falls and the risk that someone outside a car will fall prey to criminal activity.

Rockaway Beach Shell was in the not rural enough for self-service column and employed trained gas jockeys. My attendant was an experienced, stern-looking fellow with eyes as hard and cold as the round plastic buttons on his smock. He held the hose. I was careful not to slip and fall on my way back from the washroom. His look made me suspicious he was about to lay one on me. You rich motorcycle bastard, gallivanting around wasting fossil fuel. I prefer delivery trucks and contractor vans—purposeful vehicles, not squanderers. But I will service you. It is my duty under Oregon law.

The gentleman handed me the hose. Bikers don't tolerate others pumping gas into their machines.

Think of me as an explorer, please, sir. Not a gadabout. A seeker, witnessing change, like the eventual demise of gas stations. Did you know scientists abandoned the Cosmological Constants Theory? Will Oregon EV customers be allowed to plug their vehicles in themselves? Is there not a danger of electrocution?

I glanced across the street and gazed upon an uninspired display of graffiti. Hooligan spray paint art on a concrete retaining wall. Crude suggestions. Calls for society and fossil fuel sellers to go fuck themselves.

I always wonder, Do the authors really believe there's a chance their slogans may stir things up and change the world order? Their incoherent ramblings will succeed where the UN failed? What are they thinking, those who delight in violating surfaces meant to be silent? Little Grendel graffiti punks.

My attendant looked away. The graffiti was a pointless display of frustration. Misfits who took up spray cans rather than two-wheelers.

In front of the wall, litter. Along the curb, wrappers, rags, containers, spray cans, slime, and dog shit.

"A mess." I pointed with my head.

The gentleman nodded.

"Thanks," I said when the transaction was completed. "Have a safe trip."

Neuro drove off, and I thought, We are so different. He is a filler; I am a taker, a consumer. His world is static; mine in motion. He waits for arrivals; I travel to arrive. Yin and yang.

Thank heavens Neuro's tank was full. There would be no stopping us. We passed through a lowland painted a deep opal green. The road wound along a protected marsh before rejoining the 101. I trusted my GPS and let the speed limit signs guide me.

Be Flexible!

* * *

There is another kind of rider, more adept than me. Marta and Conrad, for example, are never on the brink of running out. They perpetually lend a hand with calm dignity and a grin. Graffiti does not rattle them. They possess highly developed motorcycle minds and a light heart.

My mind gets bogged down. It stumbles over blind faith and mumbles to itself. The good news? The further I ride, the better I become at just riding.

As a bend straightened out, light pressure on the handlebar returned Neuro to vertical. I leaned to enter the next right-handed curve. For nearly ten miles I was smooth, carving out left and right sweepers effortlessly.

My Motorcycle State of Mind: Unencumbered.

Slanting sunshine dappled the Pacific Ocean. A mist of insects buzzed across the sand, bound together, always traveling in a pack. I saw amorous ducks and a young couple strolling hand in hand. The road can make you think about companionship, home, hugs, separation. My mind faltered. I saw families on the beach, and a consequent feeling of loneliness grew upon me. My State of Mind became droopy.

It happens. You gotta go, but everyone wants to slide into home plate. You can't stay away forever. Come on home.

As I drove, I looked for the beauty. Marta says it's everywhere. All you have to do is open your eyes. "A motorcycle is the best seat in the house. No need to ascribe a higher meaning to what you see. God is in everything, so everything is beautiful."

I gave it a shot.

My Motorcycle State of Mind shifted to Cuddled.

* * *

The exterior of the building looked solid and inviting. After a full day of riding, I rewarded myself by climbing off and finding reassurance in a motel room.

My room was small and austere, furnished with a bed, a chair, a cheap TV, a grubby microwave, and a nonworking fridge. The door lock would do nothing to discourage an intruder. The room said, the owners don't care. A few framed pictures adorned the dull walls. The one above the bed was bare. Only the frame remained. A strip light revealed a ceiling with an industrial spray covering and a giant water stain. A dog barked and the guest in the neighboring room turned up their TV. Would Bear pound on the wall? Make my day!

I glanced out the single pane window, which was fixed so it couldn't slide more than one inch. A stranger stared in. I looked out at Neuro. The parking lot's OK? That Oddball isn't bothering you?

Cheap motel rooms have blinds installed to prevent parking lot stalkers from looking in at portraits of other lives. I drew the blinds, and the room dissolved into a dark gloom. I opened them. The stranger looked at me.

The sidewalk rolled upon the smooth slope of the earth. On foot, the dips and swerves were unnoticed. There's little need to pay attention—loose gravel won't hurl you into a ditch. A pedestrian won't try to kill you. Deer are peaceful. Walking is automatic. Stimulation is slow motion.

Nod or say hello when strangers stroll by. An urban explorer may return your gesture, "Dr. Livingstone, I presume?" Sidewalks are places of boundless possibilities, but they're not where you'll find strong communities of strollers. Walkers commiserate on park trails or at viewpoints on the Appalachian Trail. I carried my helmet with me as I walked into town. It signaled I was a traveler, not a loiterer. Perhaps I'll bump into another biker? "It's a Shoei," I'd say when asked.

"Planning to fill it with souvenirs?"

I nodded to an approaching pedestrian and attempted a Marta-like expression of delight. The stranger dropped their head. Looked away.

Tomorrow —Motorcycle Friends.

21

Rolling Stones, Rolling Wheels

On the main street of Newport, shops hawked a fine selection of goods. I poked at the art, hoping one or two pieces would start crawling to freedom. *The Great Crustacean Escape*—starring outlaw crabs fleeing their decorative prisons on custom bikes. None did, but the decorated shells were compelling. They'd make terrific conversation pieces.

"You sure have a lot of motorcycle stuff, Mike. And what's this?"

"Oregon crustacean art."

"I've heard of it. Never been lucky enough to see one with a motorcycle motif until now."

"Here's a Nova Scotia lobster claw shaped like a foot-peg."

"Nature and art. Makes a nice backdrop displayed behind my bike."

"Care for a saltwater taffy?"

I contemplated buying the tiny shells to surprise the Tony's gang at Christmas. Wouldn't anyone be thrilled to receive crustacean art?

I seldom buy mementos. Maybe a cap or shirt because they're functional. I now find junk that is not useful for motorcycling burdensome. But Newport was giving me reason to reconsider. Newport was making me reconsider my anti-knickknack stance. *Marta, my raison d'être, is to amass a renowned art collection, all tracked down on-motorcycle. Something to pass on when my tank runs dry.*

Truthfully, I'd like to clear our house of all doo-dads. Donate them to those who complain about not having enough stuff. But Dori's attached and continues to buy more. "It was on sale." "We should have a spare." "What if your cousins come?" That sort of thing.

I don't understand.

Motorcycles gradually free you from the need to be attached. They force you to pare down to essentials.

Shop bins overflowed with an abundance of saltwater taffy. I didn't count, but a sign promised:

Fifty Taffy Flavors

I'm fine with edible souvenirs. After studying all the varieties and noting the omission of a plain salt offering, I purchased two chocolate malts. I walked and chewed, using tremendous jaw power. The sticky substance stuck to my teeth when I tried to spit it out. Once extricated, it looked like the scum you don't want to find at the bottom of your oil pan. Like guilt you forgot to toss until the road shakes it loose.

The street had the cheerful, over-the-top festival vibe tourists love. No tire shops, accountants, pest control businesses, or dental offices. Tons of taffy, artwork, fridge magnets, prints, mugs, and decals. One shop was trying to unload its old postcard stock. Tape a crab to each card was my thought. It'd make a nice presentation and be a top seller.

I walked away from the retail stores, continuing well beyond the main street to a block where the businesses were modest and unattractive. If the unexpected existed in Newport, Oregon, it would be here. "Venture and ye shall find," Manny says. "Like a nomad."

A window sign jolted me. Holy Mother of Fruit Pies! Marionberry, I presume? The rare Oregon hybrid. It was like retrieving a screw knocked into one of those deep bike crevices that hoard tiny parts. Or a treasure hunter finally uncovering Yamashita's gold in the Philippines. Tomoyuki Yamashita, a Japanese WWII officer, was executed for war crimes in 1946. Fortune hunters still search for the place he hid his loot.

I had my treasure—marionberry pie. Double the cost of a Home-Run slice, because, like Yamashita's gold, it's a rarity. If you're in Newport, walk away from the tourist area to find this delight. As for war crimes, remember what Marta says: "See how things work out?" Japan refocused and now offers many fabulous two-wheelers.

After eating, I approached the tourist center using an indirect route. I was still savoring marionberry when the block took a sudden turn—from fruit pies to ladies (perhaps some men) swaggered. Several contemplated me. Vehicle sex, mister? Is that pie on your face? Saltwater taffy on your teeth? Come here, tourist boy. Don't be timid. Time for a real ride! It's the kind of sex that sticks to your teeth and you can't spit out. I continued, as casual as could be, back to the main drag. Another time, ladies. When you get a nicer van and offer a crustacean art special.

Teenagers long for vehicle sex. It's a top reason young men dismiss owning motorcycles. To me it's like comparing marionberry pie to those mass-produced syrupy round supermarket pastries. No thank you, ma'am!

Nomads of the Serengeti often have sex when they stop for water. They pump, grind, and then move on. Sometimes a partner speculates, "What if we got a real bed? Stayed put? Took out a vehicle loan? Had sex every day?" But true nomads gotta go.

I'm somewhat of a seized piston—stuck until the next itch oils the gears. My traveling rhythm requires rest and lubrication. I'd make it as far as the first Serengeti watering hole, post on social media, and then return home.

I like to travel, but not constantly. Marta says it's the maturing of the motorcycle mind. "The longer you've been riding, the more gap time you need." Part of riding is not riding. Staying put is a shot of oil on a seized spring. Suddenly the bound wire is pushing and anxious to spring again. Gotta go!

Cam says I'm just lazy. He always wants to "get a movin.'" Every trip isn't an Iron Butt marathon, Cam! I often have to undo my jacket and point at my tee shirt, the one I wear only when traveling with Cam.

Chill The Fuck Out, Cam!

Dori doesn't like me walking around with the F-word on my chest, so I wear it under something and deploy it as needed.

On another side street, two weary warriors with rugged cases rested. I crossed over to inspect. They were identical mid-sized bikes loaded with wet bags and mucky camping gear. There is an art to loading a bike, to make it comfortable with all kinds of gear strapped to it, managing hills without complaint, repacking without distress, and returning home at the end of a trip without breakage. After years of baffling organizational problems, I eventually mastered packing and abruptly stopped camping.

I felt a compulsion to wipe away the worst of the grime from the neglected machines. To distract myself, I decided to retrace my steps and acquire another slice of marionberry pie.

When I left the bakery the first time, I announced, "I'll be back," like in the movie Terminator. "I'll be back!"

The saleslady replied, "May the pie be with you."

She rides a Husqvarna FC 250.

I ate slice two as I walked back past the two forlorn camping bikes. The last time I'd packed wet camping gear, I was with Manny, Mr. Bull of the Woods. A weekend adventure I hadn't been keen on undertaking. From Tennessee, and a wilderness further south before that, Manny had become a devoted West Coast outdoorsman. Hiking. Trail biking. Hunting. Fishing. That sort of thing. I'm more of an off-the-main-drag-crustacean-art-lover type.

I remember Manny had predicted a 20 percent chance of showers. It poured, which made me grumpy as hell.

The storm gave Bull of the Woods a chance to test his new all-weather gear. He was delighted. I sulked.

"You know, if we'd stayed home, you wouldn't need any of that stuff, Manny?"

"And we wouldn't be here."

"Exactly."

"You're like my young cousin Niki. We went family camping back east in her senior year. The girl complained the whole damn time. Got on my nerves. Boy, did she hate it. Good motorcycle rider, though."

That night, around 2 a.m., Manny started buzz saw snoring.

In the morning, Bull of the Woods made coffee. "Sun's coming out. Gonna be a shiner."

I wrung water out of my towel.

"Your stuff will dry in no time."

It didn't.

We sipped. Two cups. Maybe three.

Manny told me about his cousin's adventure as a motorcycle nomad.

Niki and Nico's Motorcycle Story

Manny's cousin Niki and her partner Nico bounced between emotions like dirt bikes on rough terrain—jabbering one moment, sullen the next, then erupting in exuberance. Their spirits overflowed with the potent fuel of Gotta Go anticipation. How many more sleeps till we leave? Just common city folk about to leap across an ocean, purchase bikes, and disappear down the endless global highway.

"Transformative," Nico declared, his lanky frame projecting the determination etched into the lines of his weathered brow.

"Scary," Niki confessed, her presence suggesting someone more at home on a stage than a saddle—a dancer perhaps, with one graceful toe still planted firmly on home plate.

Nico's Tuono V4R languished in storage. Niki's F 850 was gone, along with their other possessions—sold or donated to fuel the dream. Resignation letters submitted, futures abandoned. "By god, we're really doing it," they'd say to each other.

Yet sometimes, in quiet moments, Niki wondered: Should we be doing this? They wouldn't just be changing lanes—there would be no heading home. "I'm no camper," she admitted to friends. "Maybe I'm a homebody?" But with possessions sold off and her job surrendered, she was about to become a nomad by choice. "Nico and I have each other," she reassured herself. "That's enough."

People often corner themselves into positions where retreat becomes impossible.

"Baffling," Niki's mother pronounced, head shaking in maternal disbelief. "On motorcycles? At your age? It's not too late to change your mind, dear. Let Nico go alone, if he must."

Alone? After six years as a couple? Unthinkable.

Friends peppered them with more reasonable alternatives. "What's wrong with booking a motorcycle tour? Vietnam? New England? Having jobs to return to?" The questions left even Niki disoriented. "We're going for a year. Longer if we find work. Nico can take on some work while we travel. Digital nomads."

Manny later confided, "Niki had never strayed from home for more than two weeks. Her mom—my sister-in-law—blamed Nico for planting this wild seed. I supported them quietly. Nico's solid. We'd done a few short rides together."

This wasn't impulsiveness. For two years, they had methodically researched adventure riding, devouring Long Way Down and Itchy Boots documentaries. Veterans of the road taught them about inevitable sacrifices. They spent countless hours at dealerships examining potential companions: machines under five hundred pounds before gear, dirt-road capable, mid-sized, comfortable, reasonably priced, and above all, reliable.

Their preparation was meticulous: weather patterns analyzed, insurance policies scrutinized, cost-of-living calculations made, visa requirements memorized. Vaccinations received. Budgets drawn up. They weren't married. Owned no property. Cared more for throttles than corporate ladders. Adventure wasn't just their dream—it consumed them. "It's in our DNA," they'd insist.

They planned to embrace secondary roads, camping to stretch their euros. Europe would be their training ground until they hardened.

Niki, a teacher, told her colleagues, "It's a learning sabbatical. I'll return a better educator."

"Why not just ride up to Quebec City?" friends suggested with practical concern. "It's foreign, and they speak French."

Despite her outward commitment, Niki's attempts to sever connections were sometimes half-hearted. She kept secrets. Lifelines. She harbored the uneasiness that dwells in those not born to wander. What will become of me? What have I gotten myself into?

* * *

The couple stepped off home plate during nature's rebirth—that season when the world flourishes with new possibility. When blossoms explode and birdsong fills the warming air, adventure beckons—everything about spring reenforces that we are born to be explorers. On a day when the sky stretched limitless blue above them, Niki and Nico boarded planes that would carry them from Nashville to Miami and finally to Madrid.

"You've always been my reliable one. Now my baby girl's gone," Niki's mother had murmured at the airport, her words heavy with unspoken fears.

High above the Atlantic, Nico leaned close to Niki and offered: "Be not afraid of going slowly, be afraid only of standing still." Ancient wisdom for modern nomads.

"Airplanes are a means to an end. Nothing comforting about them," Manny reflected as we huddled around the small blue flame of his camping stove.

"Cages hurtling through the sky," I agreed, warming my hands around a tin cup.

"Worse than boats, even."

"The complete antithesis of motorcycles."

"Damn fine camp coffee, though," I acknowledged, raising my cup to the Bull of the Woods.

***

They checked into a modest hotel in La Latina, a bohemian wedge of Madrid where life pressed close—stone balconies, ancient tiles, mopeds barking through narrow streets. "Shared toilet," Niki tweeted, accompanying it with a selfie. She practiced her Spanish as she sprayed the inodoro.

Nico, content with his translation app, shrugged. "On-motorcycle, we speak the same language."

The first few days unfolded like a long weekend vacation—cheap tapas, sidewalk coffee and wine, new discoveries laced with expectations of what they'd find around the corner. "Bikes will make it even better," Nico proclaimed, and on day six, they signed the paperwork.

Two identical Versys 650s—his in black, hers in white. Street-capable. Dirt-tolerant. Practical machines. The dealer sweetened the deal with a buy-back guarantee. "Your tickets home," he said with a wink.

That comforted Niki. Her bike wouldn't just show her the world; it promised to bring her back across the ocean. Mom sent pictures from Tennessee: the forsythia blooming gold across their backyard fence like sunshine bottled up and spilled.

They named their bikes. Nico called his "Atlas." Niki didn't share her bike's name. Not yet. But when she posted a picture of the two Versyses side by side, she captioned it, "A cute matched pair. Just like us."

"Living the dream!" friends replied, hearts and rocket emojis flying.

Niki wrote, "Everything we own fits on our bikes," a fragment of Janis Joplin's—*freedom's just another word for nothing left to lose.*

On day eight, like proud parents leaving the hospital, they packed their gear, snapped a photo, and pointed west toward Portugal. The sky was flawless. "We're throwing ourselves into a grand adventure," Niki's post said. "Feels surreal."

Two days of gentle roads—part highway, part secondary—just enough time to break in the engines, fine-tune packing, and test their resilience. They camped once. "Two-person tents fit one person comfortably," Niki quipped, posting a picture of Nico's boots poking through the zipper.

"We came to ride, not rough it," Nico said. Hostels became their default—less romance, more rest.

A picture from Nashville arrived—Niki's brother holding up popcorn at a Sounds baseball game. "Popcorn?" the caption read.

In Fátima, they wandered among pilgrims. In Porto, they ditched their camping gear. "Too much stuff," Niki posted. "Hostels work better." The burden of objects never feels heavier than on a motorcycle.

Their days blurred: map, ride, wander, sleep, repeat. Adventure gave way to routine, as it often does.

Then, on day seventeen, their rhythm snapped.

Nico collapsed in Santiago de Compostela—on his knees before a toilet in their pension room, fevered and wrung dry. While he slept, Niki wandered the city. She stood inside the towering cathedral where the remains of Saint James were said to rest. She spoke with Camino pilgrims—sunburnt, blistered, quiet. People at the end of journeys, about to fly home. One month. Two. A reasonable time. Niki agreed with a pilgrim group from Chattanooga. They reminded her of who she used to be.

Five days later, they rode off—not entirely on the same road.

* * *

By early July, their momentum had long since stalled. In Copenhagen, under pale northern skies, Niki and Nico moved like shadows of themselves—talking less, bickering more. The spark that had propelled them across an ocean was dead.

Life on the road, Niki decided, was not an epic—it was erosion. A perpetual state of disruption. They were worms inching forward toward some ill-defined end, worn thin by repetition and the weight of unmet expectations. "I'm homesick," she admitted to a tourist in an American-style coffee shop.

Back home, her mom sent pictures of their Fourth of July celebration. Pictures full of family and joy. Barbecue smoke curling toward Tennessee skies.

"Time to move on," Nico repeated, as if saying it would make it true. "To better motorcycle roads and real change."

But for Niki, the thought of packing up felt like preparing for a play she no longer wanted to perform.

"We're not in riding country," Nico assured her. "We're crawling. Sightseeing. This isn't what we came to do." They had detoured north so Niki could connect with her Scandinavian roots, but even that thread had frayed.

One morning over breakfast and silence—Niki spoke up. "Let's enjoy the rest of Europe and go home before winter. I'm craving stillness. Maybe if I were twenty-five. But I'm not."

She picked at her pastry. "Travel isn't liberating when it's mandatory."

"But we agreed ... at least one year."

"We also talked about being flexible."

Nico stared out the window. "We need to get to the Balkans. Ride south. Find proper roads. This isn't the journey—it's the layover."

Their disagreement flared—words hurled, feelings hurt—the kind of fight that leaves scorch marks even after apologies. It seemed they may never really speak again.

Nico fled, taking solo rides to escape the thick silence that settled between them.

Niki's mom sent more photos: Great Smoky Mountains National Park. "Had a wonderful outing," the caption read. "But nice to be back home, resting."

Home. A word Niki cherished.

"Our expectations weren't realistic," Niki said one night, breaking the quiet. "We thought we'd ride forever. What were we thinking?"

Nico answered without looking up. "Not here. Not like this." He felt like a bagger at a hill climb, bogged down, barely moving, out of place.

"Here, there. What's the difference? I just want to feel settled."

Nico heard the finality in her tone, her refusal to dream with him. He lashed out. Bitter accusations flew. Sabotage. Weakness. Betrayal.

Manny told me, "Niki said it was like watching her partner shed his old skin and become someone she didn't recognize."

In Niki's mind, the journey became the enemy. The road mocked them. Hostels smelled like failure. Her bike was a burden.

They stopped speaking. Niko rode alone. Niki walked fast and far, thinking, breathing, quietly stitching a new plan together. After confirming her teaching job was waiting, she made it final. "I'm not cut out to be a nomad. You will be better off without me. I'm ruining your dream."

A long, ragged silence followed.

They sold the white Versys in a legally murky, but necessary transaction. For Niki, it had become an anchor. They hugged—but without illusions—and Niki boarded a plane.

"I want to sleep in my own bed," she said. "Do day rides. Hike a Camino. Get a chow chow." Her mother waited at the airport, arms wide and teary-eyed. "I was scared to death," she confessed. "I kept thinking... you'd be killed over there."

"Some of us need a porch and a dog and the sounds of home," Manny said.

Gotta Go—different meaning to different people, I thought.

* * *

Nico slid into a cocoon, a tiny weekly rental, acutely aware he was living in a slot. He wondered about up and down, left and right, victory and abandonment, belonging and displacement, movement and permanence.

He drank akvavit and, when his week was up, barely got going.

"He made it to Greece," Manny told me as he topped up our coffee mugs. "To his great-grandparents' village. After the separation, he and I began trading messages. I fed him information; a substitute for Niki—I suppose. Something to fill the silence. Everyone else in the family thought there must be something wrong with the guy."

Nico's photos said, *look at me. See what you're missing, Niki. I'm with people who love me! Away, but attached. Don't you wish you had persisted?*

"Enthusiasm can lead to misadventures," Niki warned her friends.

Nico was in Croatia for the final weeks of the motorcycle touring season. "Wish we could stay and ride with you, brother," new Motorcycle Friends told him. "You're a lucky man." His new buddies had to return to jobs and steady lives. Early October, when tourists leave, what do explorers do?

Swimsuits were hung on lines for the last time. A new set of travelers appeared. They had little enthusiasm for wayward motorcyclists and no inclination to stray far from the beaten path.

"Getting ready to push on," Nico wrote.

"Moving on to?" Niki checked photos and thought Nico's face was like the autumn sky, overcast one moment and bright the next.

"Christmas in Africa!" Manny repeated Nico's declaration. "Riding a new continent. It made me want to pack up and join him."

Then Niki unexpectedly popped a question. "Why not come home for Christmas?"

It's an unfair question. Who doesn't want to be home for Christmas? The Spanish version of ♪*Oh come, all ye faithful, joyful and triumphant*◊ played on the streets of Malaga. ♪*I'll be home for Christmas. You can count on that*◊.

New Year's is for nomads. Christmas is for family.

***

When Nico arrived home, immediately it seemed all wrong. Infuriated with himself, he walked around with his right arm pumping air like

Archangel Gabriel seeking answers. He believed he'd fallen into a trap. It bewildered him. What has become of me? He watched for a sign. What you want from me?

At times, there is a veil of grief upon his face, Niki thought. Then a stillness and mystery. He is not the man he was.

When you are nomadic, it's unsettling not to move.

Nico dillydallied from room to room in his parents' house. It was clean everywhere. Quiet and empty everywhere. He missed the comfort of the Versys's drone and the constant change it brought. No one paid attention; only Nico had noticed the stillness. It's all wrong.

His parents thought his travels must have been rough. Their son needed rest. Time to catch up. Eat home-cooked meals. Make inquiries. Settle down. Fit in.

Nico felt he was in danger of wasting away in the seclusion of a home, confined until his dying day, recalling the ripple of tires on asphalt, the glint of the sun, the wind, the engine's soft vibrations.

Nico made up his mind to do something—something startling, something rash, something desperate, whatever it took to shake himself loose. He was going to break free. Rise from the muck.

"I can't do it," he announced. "I can't be here."

It shocked his parents. Niki shuddered. "I don't understand." But she did. She understood he had to go.

"Early in the new year, he left for Africa," Manny told me. "We haven't heard from him since."

A true motorcycle nomad, I thought. Some part of me envied him.

"Maybe dead?" Manny said.

Either way, he went where he needed to go.

Marta, my revolvement: Understand, the road is not endless. Like Stu, I need a Perfect Sleeper.

22

Driving Blind

Imagine a blind man driving a motorcycle. He might manage for a time, but it wouldn't be pretty—constantly one tire rotation from disaster. A lack of coffee had me driving blind. ♪Coffee. Coffee. BLACK. BLACK. In California◇.

My top box lock had been giving me trouble. It required coaxing. Just the right amount of pressure in the right spot, otherwise the mechanism wouldn't release. My mind behaves like my top box when it isn't fed a shot of morning caffeine.

I stabbed myself, twisted the blade to spread the wound, reached in, and squeezed. One at a time, I stretched each arm and leg. I bent my neck back and forth. Up and down. Again, each arm and leg. I stood on the pegs, hollered, and took deep breaths of ocean air. I sat.

♪Coffee. IN CALIFORNIA. BLACK. BLACK. In California◇. I was spitting distance from the border.

In front of me, the clouds drew apart and then massed together, lying thin and straight and then heavy and thick. As I passed a broad estuary, the wind grew stronger. A sudden and violent squall shook Neuro. Then the sun leaped into an opening and shone its beam on us.

It switched my State of Mind to Symphonic.

"Riding is like conducting an orchestra," Marta says.

"But I'm tone deaf."

"Not on-motorcycle, not if you focus. Everyone can be a maestro."

It's hard to focus when you crave coffee. Can you imagine a conductor without caffeine? The racket! The racket! The missed notes, the poor timing! Where are my ear plugs?

On the outskirts of Langlois, some jackass had chained a dog to a tree. I slowed but was down the road before I could formulate a plan. Looking back, I thought I saw a tail wagging, proof of the canine's disposition. No doubt the kind-hearted owners were coming with food and a pat. You shall be released! My guilt relieved, I wagged a leg to wish the mutt well.

The distinctive smell of the ocean grew fainter and eventually died out. Suddenly it was back. I could see seaweed waving in submarine currents. Then back to the forest, trees colored by the morning light. Creatures came and went unseen—the constant ebb and flow of infinitesimal life underwater and in the undergrowth.

"Observation," Marta says. Notice how each tree differs from the next. Why does one utility pole lean more than the others? "It's an important part of a road trip." It's easy to ride too many miles at high speed and see the road as nothing more than a long black strip of asphalt.

I tried to notice small things. The dirge always returned. BLACK. BLACK. COFFEE. How much further to coffee, for Christ's sake? I've never been an ardent fan of symphonic music.

I estimated less than half an hour. More if I returned to rescue the chained dog. Why isn't PETA on the job? Must I do everything? Music producers, please overhaul orchestral music. Lordy, lordy, my mind had sunk into a coffee-less abyss.

Then, there it was. My savior! A coffee wagon on the outskirts of town. With bright umbrellas and seating.

I deviated and ordered an Americano with an extra shot. Excellent choice! "Welcome to California," the barista said.

"Fuel," I told the owner. "As important as gloves and a helmet." We chatted and I was blessed with a free refill. Drip this time. Dark roast. Black. I got the lowdown on the beans and the roast. "Consider adding pie," I suggested, trying to be helpful. The businessperson had those puck-like muffins and a few pieces of grubby crustacean art for sale. "Get some with motorcycles and I'll be a buyer next time through."

The owner grabbed a tiny crab, wiped thick dust off its shell, and drew a decent motorcycle with a felt pen. "That'll be twenty-one fifty."

When my payment was refused, I dropped two emergency bills into an old-school tip jar.

My Motorcycle State of Mind: Fully Charged.

The names on the signs:

Pacific Shores

Jedediah-Smith Redwoods State Park

Del Norte Coast Redwoods State Park

Napa

Options to ride this way or that. I pulled over to offload coffee behind one of several signs that contained the word "Redwoods." All great explorers leave their mark—some with flags, some with footprints. Me? I christened the ground just as Shackleton did in Antarctica.

The wheels are round and they roll, I repeated as we continued south toward Crescent City. The Zen and the Art of Motorcycle Maintenance author rode west from Grant's Pass to Crescent City. I thought it would be appropriate for me to do the same route, but in the opposite direction.

"Makes a lot of sense," Den said when I revealed my plan at Tony's, "that you travel in the opposite direction."

"Because it makes no sense," Earl said.

"Exactly," I said.

In the book, the author writes about his quest to understand quality. It was his raison d'être; he had a tough time nailing it down. While Robert Pirsig was contemplating, in 1979, his son Chris was murdered outside the San Francisco Zen Center. There were rumors of insanity. "I must tread carefully," I wrote. "It may be best if I don't adopt a raison d'être, Marta."

Like Mr. Pirsig, motorcycle travelers featured in books are all on quests; most often they seek to find themselves. Sometimes they want to solve a riddle (like what is the essence of quality) or to forget a part of their past. We're all a little blind when we start out—that's how real journeys begin.

PART THREE: GOTTA RETURN

23

Home Isn't The Finish Line

"Each mile should be like a beacon on the road toward discovery," Marta says.

Marta's words are waylaid by the humdrum of travel. JOY is intermittent. MAGIC unreliable. That's why we have distractions—coffee, music, rest stops, throttle locks, intercoms. Discovery alone doesn't cut it.

More Marta: "When it fails, take a break. Don't dive into the shallow end. Head home. Home is a beacon."

Cam's take? "Suck it up."

Conrad? More measured: "Pointing your bike toward home base sends mixed signals."

He's not wrong. Home signifies the end. The point at which you stop exploring. Imagine Shackleton's return. I'm sure he was eager to play with his kids, take out the garbage, and be grounded. But, like Nico, he struggled with staying put. "Gotta go again, Em."

"Shipwrecked and frozen, and you're still not staying home? Will it ever end?"

"It was nice getting back and being together, but I must continue my quest. Exploring is what I do."

"Really, Ernie," Emily said. "This is how you treat us?"

No doubt Mr. Guilt burdened Shackleton, yet he could not deny his calling. He gave his wife a hug and was ready for trip number three.

It's a cycle. The best prep for riding is not riding. Even nomads need a home base.

When I made the turn, a note of melancholy grandeur settled in—the beginning of the end—the road home. One moment you're riding into the unknown, collecting miles like seashells. The next, you're retracing your steps. The horizon stops inviting you forward—it starts pushing you back. Even the wind changes its tune. It whispers about overdue obligations and inboxes and cracked laundry tiles.

I would run out of road, but was I done? Was my trip too short, like abandoning chemotherapy partway through? Or Sir Ernest turning north at Elephant Island. Lewis and Clark stopping in Idaho. I wasn't fully gratified, but hey—reality doesn't care. You must do this, not that. Go here, not there. The real world is in charge, not motorcycles. Bikers have homes, jobs, and obligations.

In 1969, Flight Command told the Apollo 11 crew, "You can't stay on the moon forever, fellas." It was time for Neil Armstrong to head home, potentially to be cremated alive entering Earth's atmosphere. Every member of the crew longed to return, but they felt trepidation. They had to roll the dice.

Bikers don't have a Ride Command. Outlaws do whatever the hell they like. A troublesome voice buzzed in my mind: Go rogue, Mike. Turn your back on home base. Become a true nomad like Nico. Ride to the depths of the wilderness, the empty plains, and the desolate hills. Travel to the edge of the world and then hitch a ride on SpaceX to Mars. Return home later. I enjoy putting my feet up and hanging out at Tony's. Still, the gypsy motorcycle thoughts persist.

It swells in me, this desire to explore, before being quieted by mundane realities. If only it weren't for that Tuesday appointment, the bank account, the oil sale, the stalled work project. And the unwatched series waiting at home. Most of all, there is family, the opposite of alone on two wheels.

Yin and yang.

Balance can be a pain in the ass.

* * *

Neuro descended through majestic mountain scenery into the City of Grants Pass. Shortly before seven o'clock, with a discount offer loaded on my phone, I marched into a motel lobby to be greeted by no less than General Ulysses S. Grant! It was like checking into St. Peter's Basilica in Vatican City with a coupon. About the statue, the desk clerk advised, "Ulysses never fought, explored, or lived in the area. But he's revered."

Kind of like erecting a motorcycle statue inside a Ford factory. "The general makes a fine statue." It's a rich experience to stay in accommodation with a sculpture. The lack of geographic relevance didn't diminish it one bit. Where I live, statues were being torn down. Our city council judges history by today's standards. Boy, does it piss them off. No statues of white colonizers in our city! Earl is following up on our suggestion, "Replace the statues with classic motorbikes."

Grants Pass is agreeable. But the clerk told me, "It's becoming too big, too fast."

Neuro ran into a bit of Road Vomit on the way in.

After dropping my bag in my room, I returned to put Neuro's cover on. Mile by mile, the trip had sealed our bond. We appreciated each other as people learn to live with a pet, to dwell on what is good and shut their eyes against all that is not congenial. We are united, Neuro and I—until I buy another bike, of course. Plus, the top box lock situation was really starting to get my goat.

As with pets, riders and their machines can be separated. It's the cycle of life and motorcycle marketing. With the exception, perhaps, of Marta. "As long as I breathe, Guzzi will be on the road." As a second bike.

I took time to put Neuro's cover on perfectly.

Perhaps the gentleman watching me attend to my machine noticed our bond and was touched by it. He was getting along, as they say. Grey-trimmed beard. Fuzzy mustache. Enormous eyebrows that almost obscured his vision as he stood regarding us with folded arms. "Used to ride myself," he said, patting his chin. He said he was from Southern California and, after reading Neuro's plate, said, "British Columbia?"

"Victoria."

Gunnar, the man's name was, had visited the island before the statue removal craze. He may have seen Captain Cook, Sir John A. Macdonald, and the rest of the imperfect white colonial cunts. Gunnar was not on his motorcycle at the time. "Last ride? Rocky Mountains—twenty years back. Sky so wide you could fall into it. My last bike was a blue Kawasaki Vulcan Voyager. Sold it to a retired motorcycle cop. Had Harleys, Beemers, Hondas, you name it."

I nodded to assure him I could make out the words in his scratchy voice. "Retired, you say?"

"Cops need therapy after being smacked around on the force."

Again, I nodded. "He was a motorcycle cop?"

"One of the good ones. A dream job."

When the man quizzed me about Neuro, I knew he was solid.

"Miss it," Gunnar said about his motorcycling days. "You know it's time when you drop your bike and can't pick it up." Time to become part of a bus tour group. "From bike to bus. Aging is about giving stuff up." He chuckled. "We're heading to the Boeing factory for the free tour, then back to LA."

As Gunnar showed me a photo of his tour group clustered around Ulysses, I had a raison d'être brainwave. I will not take a seat on the bus. No doubts. This is my line in the asphalt.

"Strange, don't you think? The statue?" "We're a long way from Mississippi."

According to Gunnar's tour leader, the city name honors General Grant's success at Vicksburg during the American Civil War.

"Still, it's odd."

"Maybe Ulysses got out this way after the war?"

"What if the town founders had been Portuguese?"

"It'd be Vasco da Gama Pass, and Vasco would be standing in the lobby."

Gunnar laughed. I smirked.

Gunnar grew up in Minnesota, near the home of the cop to whom he sold his Vulcan. "A donation, really." On a bench outside the lobby honoring General Grant, Gunnar told me the story of his last motorcycle. "Sold it to Officer Jim."

Gunnar's Motorcycle Story

"Never thought I'd go down." How many times had Jimmy Lowery heard those exact words? More than a hundred?

"Smarten up. Don't climb on, and you won't end up in a box." This from a guy who rode five days a week, every day, year after year. Officer Jim drove Harley Road King police bikes. The machines' care and upkeep was in the hands of civilians. Jim completed pre-ride inspections only. "It's a tool of the trade. That's all. Like my service revolver. No different from a radar gun, Breathalyzer, or coms system. I don't service them either."

Jim scoffed at Zen and the Art of Motorcycle Maintenance thinking. He wouldn't stand for anyone, Buddha included, riding along. Not on a police bike—against regulations. His Road Kings were nuts, bolts, hardware, and software.

On the job, it had been impossible to refute the harsh realities of life. "Shit happens. It's a certainty." Wind therapy does not extend to police bikes.

Officer Jim had placed blankets over deceased bikers. Rolled out yellow caution tape. POLICE LINE—DO NOT CROSS. Shrugged calamity off—it's a learned skill. On occasion he heard, "Pig on a bike!" He'd throttle up his Road King and drive away. On foot, you can't do that. "Defund the police! End the brutality!"

The wind carries away taunts.

"Sensory overload," Jim told his wife, June. "Surprising what you see on a motorcycle. Much more than in a squad car. You're plowing right through the shit, boots exposed."

At home, the couple lived in a sanctuary of domestic bliss. They supported one another and had no regrets. Their home was a refuge beyond the reach of societal missteps. In a sense, both were teachers; it was a condition of life that suited them.

Jimmy the Rider, the boys on the squad, called their mate, thanks to his incident-free record. Twice a year, Officer Jim instructed rookies at the academy. "An escape from the mean streets." A cherished opportunity to share knowledge and experience. Jimmy the Teacher, the squad joked. He had a way of connecting the structural forces of driving on two wheels to riding smart. "It's all about accident avoidance." When Jim lectured, his cheeks would flush and his eyes widened and grew bright. His audiences paid attention.

"You'll scare the motorcycle bejesus out of these newbies," the training supervisor joked.

Officer Jim grinned—he was proof accidents didn't have to happen. Thirty years. Thousands of miles. Not a single incident.

The motorcycle cop was a coveted speaker at civilian functions as well. History lent credibility, and Jimmy had loads of entertaining anecdotes. "The term 'motorcycle involved' always makes me cringe," was his opener. "People ask, is there a commonality, a preventable cause? Sure! Simple. Don't climb on. Take the bus … way safer. If you must ride, choose to be an expert."

"Ensure your medical insurance is paid up and your will is in order," Officer Jim told recreational riders. "On a bike, you're a prey animal."

"Get their attention, then educate," June coached her husband.

"Close with an amusing real-life story. On the stage, you're a showman, not a cop, my dear. You don't want to come across like a hard-nosed jerk."

At the end of each function, Jimmy the Rider rode off on his Road King. Textbook form, of course.

Jimmy retired at age fifty-three and put his work tools away—no more Road Kings, helmets, and gloves. June texted her sister: "Already restless."

The couple celebrated with a Tuscany vacation. Jim sent a text to his pals on the squad, "Scooters everywhere. No Road Kings." The following year, they toured Croatia by car. "Loads of bikers on Beemers and Piaggio Zips. No Road Kings." At times he pictured himself riding through city traffic on a naked Road King, turning heads.

June carried on working as a substitute teacher. Friends saw the couple as a glimpse of perfection. Their lives were appallingly snug.

Jimmy remodeled the bathroom and walked Spike, their puggle. The local Harley dealer offered Jimmy the Rider a part-time job. "After everything I'd said about recreational riding, I don't dare." Jimmy declined, but he began reading online motorcycle articles. "Just keepin' an eye on the industry," he told June when she noticed. "Professional curiosity."

After all, I am an expert.

There were invitations to present at motorcycle functions. "Volunteerism." "I'll need a motorcycle. Not a police bike, but a similar tool."

"You're too young to retire," June, who was grasping how annoying a bored househusband can be, pointed out.

A friend recommended he leave a note on the local riding forum. "Ex-cop. Looking for a like-new used touring bike. You may get a deal ... along with some crude suggestions."

* * *

"Jimmy posted, and I answered," Gunnar said proudly. We sat on a bench beside the motel entrance nibbling Dad's Cookies. Gunnar had several packages stuffed in his coat pocket. "A tour freebie." He insisted I accept a package of Dad's for later.

I asked Gunnar why he stopped riding.

"Arthritis. Pretty much everything's wonky. Couldn't come close to picking Big Blue up." He laughed as if his decline was a joke. "You hit eighty-five, and it's like throwing a rod."

I did the math—my age minus eighty-five.

"Sure miss it ... riding." Gunnar bit into a Dad's oatmeal raisin and then said, "Jimmy told me the first thing he noticed about me was my clothes. They were far too big. He was right, I was a larger man once. Good cop work! Jim said he noticed that when I walked, I tread on my trouser cuffs." Gunnar finished his cookie and said he could get his hands on free tour juice cartons.

"I knew Jimmy was the perfect person for Big Blue. It's kinda like I'm still riding ... thanks to Jimmy's trip reports."

The bike was a low-mileage, seven-year-old blue Kawasaki Vulcan Voyager, complete with OEM luggage and a Garmin GPS. Gunnar gave Jimmy "a hell of a deal" because he liked the idea of Big Blue in the hands of an ex-cop. No one had ridden Blue for four years.

* * *

"Like winning the squad meat draw," Jimmy told June. "It's nothing like a decked-out Road King. Don't feel like I'm on the job."

Big Blue came with a lifetime of road stories. Gunnar had toured much of North America and Europe and, like Jim, was accident-free.

Gunnar threw in all the gear he'd collected over the years. Jimmy started by studying the service manual. Domestic duties were soon ignored in favor of changing fluids, checking adjustments, and detailing. At no point in his life as a cop had he been known to sing. Now June heard humming coming from the garage. She suspected it was God Bless America.

"One hell of a deal," the cops at the station agreed. "But shouldn't you have gotten a Road King?"

"I'm not a cop anymore."

* * *

Swede, Jim had renamed Big Blue in honor of his friend even though Gunnar admitted, "Born in Minnesota."

"I'm excited about going on my first out-of-towner," Jimmy told Gunnar. "Maybe I'll ride Swede to Minnesota one of these days."

Soon he was riding solo to speaking engagements, often in neighboring states. "You're gambling with another's life," he used to say about riding two-up, but he thought it'd be nice if June came along. He was a prince about calling home at least once a day.

Five hundred to a thousand participants at each gathering. The organizing committee always reserved a room for Officer Jim. At the closing ceremony, Jimmy the Teacher smiled for the camera. The event manager presented an appreciation gift. Icing on the cake. He enjoyed the ride, the attention, and being accepted as a member of the community.

There were questions about the Vulcan. "A very nice elderly gentleman entrusted it to my care," he explained. Sometimes he told a Gunnar story.

At Morning Coffee with Officer Jim, questions were predominantly about entrapment. How to fight speeding tickets. Seldom did attendees request safety tips. Jim normally had a couple of drinks at the beer garden or local pub to mingle; there were always "Buy you a beer, Officer Jim?" invitations.

Hundreds attended his formal presentations.

"Prevented an accident or two," he'd assure June when he returned, but he had no idea really. Still, shit happens.

"Worked for years but never really rode," he confessed to Gunnar. He'd return from one event and soon got an itch to ride to the next one.

* * *

Following a rally sponsored by a Christian motorcycle club in late July, Officer Jim rode west, heading home. He enjoyed Gotta Return; never had thoughts about following the never-ending highway. "Good Christians," Jim told June. "They don't preach or question my road to salvation."

According to Garmin, six hundred and nine miles lay ahead of Swede. On secondary highways. "You're not on patrol anymore, Jimmy. Explore," Gunnar advised.

For experts, riding is instinctual and automatic. Jimmy doubted there was a situation he couldn't get out of or at least minimize the consequences of. He was at ease on Swede.

The two-lane highway meandered up a series of rolling hills, bending with the contours of the land. Small puddles from the previous day's rain lay beside the asphalt. The big blue machine was rock solid, mastering everything in its path.

Jimmy checked for a suitable photo spot. Gunnar would be waiting for trip information. "Too bad we never got to ride together, Jimmy."

"We can," Jimmy said one day. He aimed to ride two-up on Gunnar's birthday. "We'll bend the rules."

"Needn't worry about risking my life. If I drop dead in the saddle, it'd be a dream send-off."

Jimmy regretted his Road Kings never made it out of town. No trips. No photos. Always trapped.

At the crest of a hill, Swede pulled over. Without air movement, the heat was oppressive. A few darting flies ignored the sun. A meal! A meal! They wanted blood. Riders with gear aren't good targets.

Not a stunning view, but a reasonable backdrop for the star, Big Blue. Two pics with a rambling note. Jimmy edited as he walked back and forth across the gravel pullout, waving his arms at the mosquitoes. A pickup truck passed, headed east. A father with his kids. Jimmy reduced his erratic movements and managed a casual wave. The truck honked. Swede pulled out.

* * *

"Nature's raw beauty," he'd written in his message. "Colors seem to burst from deep within hills and the rolling landscape." Jim enjoyed writing in a way that was nothing like a police incident report. "I was told at the rally, roads snake their way around the world, begging to be explored. Let the earth beneath your tires define your days."

Gunnar thought it was over-the-top, but he was tickled. Big Blue was helping Jimmy the Cop break out.

Jim hummed "You're a Grand Old Flag." The Vulcan accelerated downhill toward a tight right curve. Trajectory locked in. Weather hot but fine in the wind. No oncoming traffic. Nothing in the rearview mirror. No wildlife. The road well maintained without potholes, gravel, or other hazards.

The bike swept through the first sweeper, its wheels hugging the road, leaning at the perfect angle—a flawless execution. Some think big boats like Road Kings and Vulcans can't take corners. Jimmy smiled.

Swede exited the next curve and began straightening up, but then stumbled. For a second, the driver surrendered control. Something coated the surface. Oil brought up by rain from the previous day? Jim's adrenalin spiked. Swede slowed and pulled over. Don't ride when you're tense. "Get off your bike. Shake it off," he told audiences. "It'll only take a minute and may save you from becoming roadkill."

Jimmy recalled a Christian rider telling a story about going over the bank of a similar hill. "Happened in the blink of an eye. Like being hit by a bullet, one moment you're whole, the next you're wounded in the fight of your life. The edge of the road was about thirty feet above me. A sharp rock poked me in the back ... that's the first thing I was conscious of."

Try to stay calm. You'll be alright. How often had Officer Jim repeated those words at the scene of an accident? But it's impossible not to panic when death sniffs at your boots, waiting to set its claws into you.

"I lay motionless on the slope of that hill, waiting," the Christian had said.

For what? A miracle? St. Christopher to appear? Navy SEALs to descend from a Sikorsky SH-60? A stray police Road King?

"The pain was like a rollercoaster... overwhelming, then easing off.. I heard a large truck pass. It didn't slow. I was way below the crest of the hill, completely out of sight. Didn't know where my bike ended up ... my phone was in the tank bag. I prayed." The believer looked at the safety expert as if to say, You can't teach devotion, buster. Not in a safety course. "I was in the hands of our Lord."

When shit happens, it's a blessing to believe.

"I crawled up that hill, fighting for each inch, pulled by my faith."

Jim looked down the slope of the hill and wondered, If I'd gone over just now, would my experience save me? Are discipline and determination as strong as faith?

"The first car didn't even slow down. It was a motorcycle group that stopped—Harleys with loud pipes. They looked like Hells Angels." He laughed. "One was a medical doctor. Safety isn't enough, Jim. You must believe."

Jimmy did a high knee march across the pullout and climbed back on. As he drove, the ex-cop wondered about the metaphysics, the Zen of motorcycling.

* * *

"Are you a religious person, Gunnar?" Jimmy was on his second plate at the Country Gardens lunch buffet. He explained riding had him wondering, Was there a big bang? Is there a holy trinity? Are we part of a birth-life-rebirth cycle? Questions old Officer Jim never reflected on.

"Why is there anything? I used to wonder when I rode. Why is there Minnesota, or surströmming, or an opioid epidemic? It can make your head spin." Gunnar smiled. "Doesn't happen on bus tours. Mostly I just fall asleep. But I have wonderful memories. I look out the window and imagine I'm on-motorcycle." He stood. "Dessert, I think. Apple pie? Two slices?"

Jimmy nodded. He had a way of combining starchy syrupy buffet pie into a single slice of somewhat honest pie.

Gunnar had Dad's Cookies.

In Jimmy's car, on the way home, Gunnar sang: ♪Yippie-yi-o. Yippie-yi-yay Ghost Riders in the Sky◈.

Jimmy the Rider hummed along.

That night, I sent a note to Marta. "A revolution—we will ride at eighty-five, a road trip."

Gunnar copied me on his message to Jimmy. It included a photo of me standing at attention beside General Ulysses S. Grant and one of Neuro. Gunnar's comment read, "One of us."

Good gravy, I thought. The road just introduced me to my motorcycle sage.

24

Disconnected, But In Gear

The soothing motion of two wheels can lull riders back to the womb. Not yet exposed, without expectations, and weightless. At Tony's, we call it being disconnected. The topic always produces a lot of "come on's," "get real" eye rolls. It's farfetched, but where my mind goes and how well my body manages motion with little conscious thought surprises me.

There are times I don't seem to be driving. All the necessary operations are performed, triumphing over the overwhelming realities of physics, shoving aside the puzzling tenets of being human. It's a curious phenomenon, this cooperation between machine and rider. The times I become disconnected from thought, but deeply tethered to instinct. The way a hawk floats without flapping. It's not just wind therapy. It's a temporary surrender.

Back in the womb?

Yin-yang?

My Motorcycle State of Mind: The wheels are round and they roll.

"Autopilot is essential for jets but goes against everything motorcycles stand for," Conrad says. "Bikes require constant conscious decision-making. Wombs are for babies not yet on their quests."

"Keep your eye on the road."

"And your hands upon the grips."

"Even the sun is trying to kill us." Dolores is predisposed to melanoma. It worries her more than crashing.

"Proximity awareness."

Disconnectedness the gang understands, but back in the womb might be a mile too far.

Sometimes I kid Marta. Over the intercom, "Hey Marta, you back in the womb?"

* * *

The weather was uncertain. It threatened to be miserable, cloudy, and raw with a penetrating dampness; even the birds looked worried. But over the next hill, it was pleasant. The temperature warmed, and the clouds parted. The birds sang and enjoyed themselves immensely. Except the vigilant, who feared attacks by gangs of avian avivores circling kill sites.

I caught sight of a motorbike coming toward us. As its definition grew, I noticed it was one of those two-wheelers that looks like it should be in a pack, like football teammates or chorus line dancers. It was exhilarating to see it cut loose. I waved—Hi there, lone rider! Have you been in the womb? Ride safe!

There was a brief connection. Dr. Livingstone, I presume?

I thought: It's a shame I'm not capable of Marta-type waves. I did my slightly extended glove wiggle.

Oh well. We passed, and I didn't care.

Songs and ocean scents were in the air. The clouds shifted, casting light and shadows. Mile after mile, the scene transformed. The sky winked, and the Long Tom River rolled along as lazily as time itself. We were on a road between the interstate and the coastal highway. This is the new frontier, the land between major highways.

One fact was certain: in the open air—clear, cold, hot, blinding, and dull—there was constant change.

When Marta said, "The wind talks to those who listen," Conrad asked, "What if you're in the womb?"

I listened to the wind and looked at the Long Tom, flowing, remarkably detached from tribulations.

My Motorcycle State of Mind: Flowing Like a River.

This state of Disconnectedness does not come to me through effort, practice, skill, or meditation. On-motorcycle, it is possible to instill a subtle, quiet enthusiasm. It is beyond science and found only by those in balance.

The wheels are round and they roll—ride, be receptive, and it may happen to you.

Before me lay a splendid, satisfying sweeper with an easy transition into another curve. Trepidations of direction are welcome on motorcycles. They require a response and pull their captains back to the bridge.

After a steep climb to the freshest air, Neuro slipped down the other side, gravity performing the lion's share of the work.

Further north, the country through which the road meandered was rich and beautiful. The weather was fine. The traffic was sparse.

Then, abruptly, like Rip Van Winkle awakening from his slumber, two lanes became four. And then more, as Highway 99 funneled Neuro into Portland. I sang, ♪Take It Easy◊.

Traffic devoured us. Rip Van Winkle shuddered. It's hard not to be overcome with disgust at the sight and stench of it. Road Vomit, everywhere. Open sores to be breached. Hold your breath. Grind it out.

Snail traffic surrounded Neuro, threatening to consume us like pack ice.

But on this day, the ice cleared. Neuro sprinted, and we slipped across the Columbia River into Washington State.

The interstate would lead us to Olympia and a curvy delight that follows the Hood Canal toward the Pacific. Then a left turn back to the Coho ferry. First, an hour and a half of freeway riding. I try to think of divided highways as an oasis. Freeways make fewer demands on focus, planning, defensive driving, shifting, throttle, navigating, and the rest of motorcycle decision-making. The drone of the engine and the sound of pavement rolling underneath can be calming. There are no stoplights, intersections, sharp curves, cars wanting to turn left, or pedestrians. Traffic cops hide behind overpass walls, but we know they wait.

On the I-5, I was free to speculate.
Where are the truckers headed?
Why is the Mercedes in such a hurry?
How did that cager get a license?
Stuff like that.
There were scents: freshly cut grass, plowed fields, diesel, forests.
Motorcycles love curvy roads, but interstates can be restful. At least tolerable for a short while.
Halfway to the turnoff at Olympia, my **Motorcycle State of Mind switched to: Grinding it Out.**
On an interstate, the oasis will peter out. You will see nothing of interest. As the Ass Problem intensifies, all you can do is plod along trying not to slip into dumbass autopilot or Blockhead speed-freak mode.

* * *

At my motel in Centralia, I met Marty. Marty was traveling with Peggy, a lady on a mid-sized adventure bike.
"Marty is named after my dad, who taught me to ride," Peggy said. "Now Marty travels with me." Marty tugged one way, Peggy the other, with the leash taut between them. It was a tug-of-war, master versus pet.
Peggy gave the leash a gentle jerk. The cat skidded a few inches closer. His toenails dug in, but he managed to rub himself against my leg.
I bent and petted him. I wondered what Marty identified as. Animal or biker?
"My cat, Bunny, is waiting at home." Not really. Cat states of mind don't dwell on things. I showed Peggy a picture. "He likes to rest on stationary seats. Can't imagine him riding." Peg nodded. "Got to start when they're kittens." Otherwise they're conditioned to be scaredy cats.
Dogs on bikes? Adorable. Cats on leashes, let alone motorcycles, make you wonder about their owners. They're like a custom chopper gone too far
I sent a picture of Peggy, Marty, and their bike to the gang.

Dolores replied, "Felines are fiercely independent. Maybe a perfect motorcycle fit?"

No, Dolores. It's just weird. Like Bob's friends Max and Rossi.

Marty may be an exception, but dogs are better explorers. Cats like to stay in their lane, kill birds, and bury their shit.

Dogs love to explore and run wild, giving where-to-poop norms the finger.

25

The Last Ride

Max's Motorcycle Story

My deceased Motorcycle Friend Max had a poster of Unsinkable Sam in his garage. He was fond of cats and admired Sam—even with his Nazi past.

Unsinkable started in the German navy as a ship's cat. Over the course of his naval service, Sam survived three sinkings. He started aboard the Bismarck, which HMS Cossack sank in 1941. The British crew found the feline floating on debris hours after the Bismarck went down. They took him aboard and named him Oscar.

Later in the war, a torpedo hit and sank the Cossack, killing 159 crew members. Oscar survived and was rescued again, along with the remaining crew. His last service was aboard the HMS Ark Royal, an aircraft carrier. A Nazi U-boat torpedoed the Ark Royal, and it sank the following day. The cat survived and retired to Belfast, where he lived in a seaman's home. Unsinkable Sam died in 1955, fourteen years after the Bismarck went to the bottom.

"He was a cat with remarkable biker grit," Max always said when he told the story. If warriors discovered motorcycles, would they make miles, not war? Probably not, Max thought.

Rossi was the name of Max's cat.

***

Max didn't call it his last ride.

He called it a farewell tour. "My bucket list," he told the doctor. "The only thing left on it, actually."

Max had never been a list guy. He was a rider, the kind without a GPS route cast in stone. Now he was a cancer guy too. He didn't say the word much. Pancreatic. Stage IV. Inoperable. A prognosis that came with a sharp expiry date and no options other than "arrange your affairs."

He chose to arrange a ride.

"You could end up dead on the side of the road," his doctor warned.

"Better than dead on the couch," Max replied.

"You could crash."

"So could the cancer. Doesn't mean it will."

"You could go fast in the wrong place."

"I could also go slow in the right one. Listen, Doc. I'm not asking for permission. I'm just giving you a heads-up."

Max didn't need an argument. He needed two things: a ride and someone to take care of Rossi when his ship sank.

That's when Sonny came in. A riding friend. Not too close, not too distant. Just right. A solid, no-fuss guy with an old R100 Beemer, happy to lead from the front and shut up when silence was needed. When Max pitched the ride, Sonny didn't hesitate. "I'll go," he said. "What do we need?"

"A week."

Max prepped Rosie, his Gold Wing. Big, plush, effortless. He called her his palliative care machine. "She'll get me to the Grand Canyon or see me off trying." It wasn't bravado. It was a wish.

They left in early May.

The route was loose. "Let's just head toward red rock country and figure it out as we go," Max said. Day One, he felt strong. A little pain, a little stiffness, but the wind helped. The rhythm of the road—life condensed in time—reassured him. He told Sonny, "This is it, man. This is what it's all about. Not the fight, not the fear. Just being here and ride on. Who knows what comes next?"

By Day Three, the symptoms flared. Sharp jabs in the gut. Fatigue like a heavy tent collapsing in on you. He skipped meals, took meds, hid his moans under his helmet. Sonny didn't say much, but he knew. Max's skin looked thinner. His movements, slower. When they stopped for gas, Max leaned against Rosie like a man wanting to fade into his machine with its memories.

It was just after sunrise when they parked at Mather Point in the Grand Canyon. Sonny turned to see Max already off the bike, helmet in hand, eyes fixed on the chasm.

No words—some views don't need narration.

After a minute, Max said, "You ever hear of Unsinkable Sam?"

Sonny shook his head.

"War cat. Rode three different warships. Every one of 'em sank. He survived them all. German Navy, British Navy, didn't matter. Always made it to the next thing." He didn't explain further.

Max didn't need to spell it out. Sonny knew what he meant. Some riders keep floating even after everything around them goes under. Wrecked ships, lost jobs, dying bodies—whatever. They keep riding. That was the grit Max admired. Not bravery exactly, but that quiet defiance that says: not yet. The road can give you that—just enough forward motion. Max didn't believe in miracles, but he believed in bikes. And I guess, in cats that refused to drown.

Sonny nodded. He'd promised to take Rossi when the time came.

Later that day, Max told him, "I think I'm done." They were in a motel in Flagstaff, sharing soup and ride memories. "It's what I needed. Rosie and the canyon. What more do I need?" He paused. "I want you to have Rosie."

Sonny said nothing, just raised his glass.

They rode to Phoenix the next morning. Max moved slowly, but he rode the whole way. When they reached the storage lot, he wheeled Rosie in and said goodbye. "She's yours now."

Max flew home business class. Sonny rode solo.

Three weeks later, there was a memorial ride. Twenty bikes, Sonny and Rosie leading the way. Rossi the cat peered out from a soft-sided carrier.

Max's Motorcycle State of Mind: Move over angels. I'm ready to ride with you.

At the interment, Sonny held Rossi. *He's there now—with Unsinkable Sam.*

The cat's poster was now stapled to Sonny's garage wall.

26

Read The Signs

The box was mounted on a post. Everything about it said top-notch, professional installation of extreme importance. Car drivers didn't notice the metal enclosure, but on-motorcycle it stood out like a nude Amish dancer at a barn-raising.

A peephole in the center of the box winked as Neuro passed. Or did it aim and shoot? Perhaps it was glitter from the sun? An electrical malfunction? In any event, I honked, "Hello there, Box. What have you seen today? Do you have information worth sharing? Part of a research project? Got thoughts on the state of the union? Do your batteries need charging?"

Always so many questions on-motorcycle.

A warning sign before the post may have been helpful.

MOTORCYCLES DO NOT BE DISTRACTED BY THE BOX

Had I been driving a large pickup, I'd have tied onto the post and pulled the spy box down. For the safety of motorcycles to come.

Motorcycles are not built to push, pull, and destroy. So I carried on—wishing the contraption well.

My Motorcycle State of Mind: Best Wishes, Box.

Well balanced and smooth sailing, I included in my Marta update. "I saw a deer and wished it well."

As the road snaked along the start of the Hood Canal, I looked for a spot to stop. I needed a meal before enjoying the glorious twisties that lay ahead. It was the perfect time slot. 10:57 a.m.—wide open. The grey zone—late breakfast or early lunch.

The area is oyster rich, but seafood is best later in the day. While I contemplated, I spotted a food truck in a small ocean side town. A sign advertised:

Gourmet Hot Dogs. Home of the World's Best Dog.

How could I not stop? Perhaps suggest the owner relocate to Queets beside the World's Tallest Spruce Tree? Two record holders. Bound to pull customers in. Well away from the oyster competition.

The truck had a cheerful hotdog wrap, and a framed picture of Joey Chestnut, world champion eater. He had downed sixty-three dogs and buns in ten minutes to win another Nathan's International Hot Dog Eating Contest on Coney Island. Outstanding for an average-sized man.

I was after quality, not quantity, and asked, "Which one is the best in the world?"

The cook pointed to the board. One choice was **World's Best.**

Deep-fried shredded brussels sprouts were listed as a topping.

"Bet you don't sell many of those."

"Not my top seller."

"How does Joey remain so trim, I wonder?"

"Works out."

"Like any competitive athlete."

"Wish I had his fortitude." The cook patted his belly. "It's a squeeze in a food truck."

I went with the **Cheesy Mexican** on a steamed whole wheat bun, topped with a creamy cheese sauce, red onions, peppers, tomatoes, cilantro, lettuce, crispy onions, and a dab of salsa. I agreed to hold the mustard until I tasted, and then I experienced a flavor explosion. Hands down the best dog I'll ever eat. The pleasurable experience enhanced by the anticipation of a great ride to come.

I wondered what Joey would think about my choice. Why eat one Cheesy Mexican when you could train for a championship? Wolf down two dozen plain dogs in fifteen minutes. Start building capacity.

Clearly, raisons d'être don't have to be delicate.

I'm more of a food explorer than a competitive eater.

"It can't be the World's Best Dog contaminated with brussels sprouts."

"You're not the first person to mention that."

"I'll take one of your World's Best Oat Bars," I said. "To go."

I sent a pic of my Cheesy Mexican to Tony's and announced I'd be ordering both the super expensive deerskin gloves and the miracle sealant. My State of Mind? Shoot for the World's Best. Be indulgent. Quality not quantity. I think most riders are like that. Plus, turning stags into gloves is a noble undertaking.

"Mustard?" Conrad asked.

"Not necessary." I imagined the conversation between Tony and Conrad that followed. It'd be like their, what is the world's best motorcycle, debate?

My meal was so damn good, I rode away satisfied, with no room to stop for the Out of This World Battered Oysters down the road.

Outside of town, brooding trees lined the hills—bent and stunted by rocks and relentless wind. Their branches drooped. What a terrific spot for the World's Largest Spruce Tree, I thought. Upright and tall, it would tower above the crowd, insisting tourists stop to marvel. It would dominate, like a motorcycle amongst cars on a curvy road.

Neuro rolled onto Hallelujah Road. God bless all the old-time builders who respected the lay of the land. I crept forward like a racer inching up to the starting line.

* * *

On my right, a vast watery channel wound its way to the Pacific. Earlier in the year, I may have seen transient orcas breaching on their way to open ocean. Tailed by nuclear submarines from the Bangor Base north of Seattle. Neuro crossed a marshy tract full of brush and the odd, outlandish tree twisted by its salty environment.

When we passed the township boundary, my State of Mind sang: Hallelujah!

A fitting way to wind down a trip.

Old meandering roads are brilliant as long as you can bypass impediments. Many of these roads don't have passing lanes or legal opportunities to overtake. On this highway, safety engineers opted for a workaround. Bulldoze a few pullover spots. Pound in some **SLOW VEHICLE PULLOVER** signs. Should do the trick. Except vehicles ignore the signs because slow is a relative measure. My RV corners pretty well for a thirty-eight-footer. I'll lose momentum, so I ain't pulling over. Neuro passed a dozen vehicles, one legally. What do you do when drivers refuse to comply? Write off a Hallelujah Road? Dawdle behind four-wheels? Concede to the Fully Loaded Hay Truck cornering standard? Not a chance.

If you choose, scrape your pegs!

You're under no obligation.

When I brought Marta up to date, she suggested a sign that says,

Respect Motorcycles. PULL OVER, NIMRODS!

Tony's has a few police regulars. They often hear, "Do Not Pass lines are discriminatory. Why must motorcycles only pass where it's safe for a Ford Escape or Holden Concrete truck to do so?"

"Cause you may pass a ghost car. We have an obligation to protect you from yourself."

Last time it happened to me, Marta pulled in behind my bike, took her helmet off and gave me her suck-it-up-cowboy look.

Tony says, "It's a cost of doing business."

* * *

Before I stopped for my Cheesy Mexican, I passed a sign that said:
Ecology Crew Working
Orange cones appeared first. Followed by:
Fines Doubled in Work Zones
More orange cones. Neuro crept along, but not a single environmentalist or flag person could be seen. The entire crew must have been tagging endangered Western Pond Turtles in the forest. That's a much better use of resources than:

Road Crew Working

Working at wiping out magnificent curvature.

Modern architecture and roadways share the same design principle—build them sterile, bland, and straight. Old character buildings are revered. Governments and heritage foundations pour millions into their restoration. Then we stand back, marvel, and applaud. Why is this standard not applied to highways?

"In a world of motorcycles, roads would be different," Den says.

He's right. We're riding on a tipping point. Bulldozers are being dispatched at an alarming rate to straighten and destroy.

Is our destiny to become Freeway Riders?

My Motorcycle State of Mind: Endangered.

Like the western pond turtles.

In a changing world, perhaps signs will proclaim:

Motorcycle Roads Matter!

Because we shouldn't just be commuting through life.

* * *

I raced over Hallelujah Road's glorious miles of asphalt, my riding rules tucked into my back pocket. My mind has a sweet spot: throw caution to the wind Mikey Boy—but don't kill yourself by doing something stupid. Scrape your pegs, not your body.

"Wasting a great stretch of road is criminal," Cam says.

I agree.

Marta tells Dolores, who is learning to ride, "It's not necessary to drive like Cam. Ride your ride, not his."

"What a waste," Cam whispers.

At the coast, Hallelujah Road meets interstate traffic. I turned west to join a long, slow forty-mile procession to Port Angeles. Here, dedicated passing lanes replaced pullovers. But all were clogged with cagers performing slow-motion maneuvers.

A good sign would be:

MOTORCYCLES: HUNKER DOWN AND GRIND IT OUT—CAGERS BLOCK ALL LANES.

Unless we could persuade the powers that be to erect:

CAGERS KEEP RIGHT OR BE SHOT.

The Tony's gang thinking:

If everyone rode motorbikes, problem solved.

I stared at the ocean—a narrow channel now transformed into an immense expanse. My trip was nearing its conclusion. I saw pleasure boats heading out, their journeys beginning; mine was about to end.

My Motorcycle State of Mind: Yikes!

Before the end of each trip, there should be a warning sign:

MOTORCYCLES, LAST CHANCE TO RECONSIDER AND TURN AROUND.

Would I?

It's a tough one.

I had the end-of-trip jitters.

* * *

As Neuro rolled onto the Coho, I congratulated myself. All parts done well. No giant mistakes. Every mile enjoyed, at least in hindsight. What can I take away from my trip? To merge with my other life experiences? What does it mean to live life well?

People keep swimming upstream until they lose ability or interest and then die like spawning salmon.

Marta, my revolvement: ride. Find balance. The wheels are round and they roll and that's enough.

27

Home Base

Rapturous crowds applauded Sir Ernest Shackleton. King Edward VII raised him to Commander of the Royal Victorian Order and later to Knight. The Royal Geographical Society honoured Ernest with a gold medal. His story of survival fascinated homebodies.

It was a case of The Worst Explorations Make the Best Stories. Modern motorcycle law: the worse the ride, the better the bar story. No one wants to hear about miles spent traveling down Nothingness Highway or days sailing the Weddell Sea.

Emily and the kids yawned at Ernie's endless-wave tales—like listening to someone recount three days on prairie slab. In modern times, rather than son Raymond asking, "tell us about the ice squishing your boat," he might ask, "tell us about the time your pannier broke when you hit black ice and skidded along the highway."

You pull into your driveway, unstrap a bag, and don't bother explaining what it meant—you'd fail. Motorcycling isn't a story—it's a sensation. You had to be there. And so, the adventure gets reduced to tire wear and fuel stops. The internal transformation? That's yours alone.

My dog Pearl and my cat Bunny waited. Pearl is a top-notch greeter, while Bunny does his cat indifference act.

Sure, Bunny. I bestowed joy—treats all round.

Both pets were appreciative. It's great to see you! Especially with food. What a terrific best pal!

I showed them my crustacean art. Pearl sniffed. *Don't you dare move!*

Apart from adoring pets, returning motorcyclists are in the same league as lesser-known explorers. Like Adrien Jolliet, who tramped around Michigan's Lower Peninsula in the 17th century. When he stumbled across beaver lodges, rivers of blood flowed. On his return to Quebec, his wife Jeanne asked,

"Discover anything transformational, like a new world, perhaps?"

Adrian tried to explain the importance of the fur trade to the new world economy, but gave up.

"Inutile," he said and left to go trapping.

***

I had a coffee appointment with Marta at Tony's in two days' time. 9:45 a.m., when Elena pulls cinnamon roll batch two out of the oven. Better than a brass band? I think so. Oh, the aroma. The delicious smell of steaming dough, spice, and coffee.

My Motorcycle State of Mind: Gooey.

It's necessary to acclimatize; even brief trips need recovery time. Moments to transition from explorer to stationary. I looked back with pleasure. The lines of the road, how they led my eye with a desire to see the limits of the horizon. How I felt I could go on forever. I thought about the people I'd met along the way. Were they still riding? Would Mark be at the Queets gas station if I pulled in a year or two from now? Will the HomeRun Café maintain its pie standards? Should I have purchased crab shells for the Tony's gang? Will I ride with Bear or Coach Marvin? Will Nico settle down?

My odds of dying from prostate cancer—about 3%—are higher than dying from motorcycle. Stuff like that.

Neuro was on her center stand, waiting. Steadfast. When it's time to go again, I'll be ready. It's what motorcycles do. Respect your machines; they can be trusted.

Tony says, "Cherish the things you cannot have while riding."

It's a reminder to enjoy a cinnamon roll or Tart of the Month.

I gave Bunny a gentle hug. He purred. Pearl got lots of pats. Dori and I went out for dinner.

When Columbus returned home aboard the Pinta, he soon realized, I don't miss Spanish civilization as much as I thought I would. There's a great big world out there. It was 1493. No electricity, internet, video entertainment, fast food, or other modern-day distractions. Almost immediately, he got the itch and arranged to get the hell out of Palos de la Frontera.

"Must sail back to the New World," he told his wife, Felipa. "Our king's never satisfied with his loot. Gotta go, I'm afraid."

"Weren't you supposed to be in the Orient?" Felipa replied. "You did go on and on about a shortcut to the Far East. How you'd return with tea and spices. Instead, you got lost."

Columbus muttered, "Sin punta" and grabbed his duffel bag.

I'd been home only a very short time when the itch returned. Gotta go! Gotta go! Gotta go!

"No!" I yelled. "Stay Put! For god's sake, do not go."

I took myself to Tony's for distraction. The itch abated for the duration of my visit. Cam was there eating a Cosmic Special; he gave me one of his battered pickles.

When I returned home, I said, "Cam wants to do a run to the interior."

Dori looked at me as if I'd lost my marbles.

"A long weekend is all." *Technically closer to a short week.*

She shrugged.

I shrugged.

We were on the same wavelength.

To ease the mood, I showed her a picture of Scooter Boy.

28

Lopsided or Balanced?

When I sent Tony's the pictures, the gang's response was "Lopsided?"

"Big time."

"But balanced now, you say?"

"Seems so."

I'd taken the picture at a pullover close to the end of Hallelujah Road. The proximity to home base had me mulling my trip over, mostly to sort out how to tell Marta about my decision not to have a raison d'être. Marta, my goal is to make it through life without a tangible purpose. At the pullover, I had stretched and practiced my speech. I'm a simple man, Marta. I ride when I itch. Return. Repeat. It's all I need. I've decided I don't require an overarching objective. I have a motorcycle. The ride caught me—that's enough.

Every bike leans. Every rider wobbles. Real progress happens when you're off-center. We ride because straight lines are lies.

I imagined Marta's response: Both motorcycling and life are better when there's a hill to climb.

I once met a man who told me he had no interests. I had found it shocking and unimaginably sad. But there I was, standing on the side of the road, a few miles and a ferry ride from home, having traveled and contemplated, with a blank mind.

Patty's Motorcycle Story

At Tony's, I told Cam about the three riders heading south who pulled in just as I was preparing to leave the Hallelujah Road pullout. "So I stayed put. Turns out they were a chatty trio." Patty explained they were bound for Eugene, Oregon, to attend an event. Their Facebook friend was performing.

"Scooter tricks," Patty had said. "Amazing stunts."

She held up her phone to show a baby photo of him. "He was born an ugly duckling."

She wasn't exaggerating.

"Teased and humiliated as a child."

I could see why. It's hard not to stare at deformity. The kid had an immense appendage; his left ear dwarfed his Druid features.

I told Cam, "The picture made my hand go up to check my own anatomy."

"He was a peculiar baby," Patty had said.

No, he was an ugly baby. A freak.

"A bit odd."

Grotesque. Hideous. "Rides a scooter, you say? A motorbike scooter?"

Patty played a short video of a young man performing stunts. "Impressive," I said, and meant it. From wheelies to front-tire stoppies to burn-outs to balance, this kid could make two wheels defy physics. At Tony's, I played the same video for Cam.

"He's a poster boy now." Patty showed me another pic. "See? We're friends … online. Finally going to meet up."

The young man had become merely odd-looking. Still, it was admirable, I thought, that Patty wasn't put off.

"Mind you, she's no Marilyn Monroe herself," Cam said.

"Tell me more," I had said to Patty.

Just then, Tony wandered over and joined us. 'Tell us more,' he said.

29

Saved by Cycle

The 1992 Winter Paralympics were winding down when Manfred Trent Weber set out on his adventure. There is a noble heart for newborns, but Trent made relatives gasp.

Blobfish!
Ugly duckling!
Misfit!

Despite the baby's numbing appearance, aunties and uncles said what was expected. "Such a cutie pie. Isn't he precious?" Youngsters were instructed, "If you can't say something nice, don't say anything at all."

The Webers were not a handsome family. Adding a baby with a bulging ear jutting out like a toy catcher's mitt was cruel. Getting on with Druid features and bland personalities is an ordeal. Add a kid with an irregularity and weakened parents are devastated. Beyond the offending appendage, Trent was not pleasant to look at. He resembled his grim father, with the same large eyes, dark hair, and stern features. From his mother, he inherited a pale droopiness. Life is about avoiding lopsidedness, but Manfred Trent Weber was out of whack from day one.

Mom and Dad attempted to hide the ear under bonnets, but snickers persisted about the cock-eared Weber kid.

The family sank further into the despondency of their marginal existence.

"Cauliflower Boy," kids teased at school. "Dumbo." "Cock-eared creep."

"He'll grow out of it," doctors expected, and Trent's abnormality receded as other parts developed. But the devilry of childhood misery, its dark reflections, its solemn and brooding state of mind, cannot be shrugged off.

Trent liked to read fairytales about liberation from impossible circumstances.

Rapunzel, Rapunzel, let down your hair, and Rapunzel was saved from imprisonment in a dark tower.

Fee-fi-fo-fum! Magic beans turned things around for Jack's family thanks to a beanstalk.

The wind, the wind, the heaven-born wind, the children answered. Then Gretel shoved the Witch into the oven and rescued Hansel.

Whether by Olympian effort, heroic courage, or happenstance, it is a remarkable mystery how the baffling puzzle of life can unexpectedly transform. In our time, Beatle Paul and Beatle John found one another. Steve Jobs and Steve Wozniak started Apple. Wayne Gretzky picked up a hockey stick.

At age fourteen, Manfred found his magic under a tarp at the back of his grandpa's garage—a 1979 Harley Shovelhead. The boy climbed on and daydreamed about being carried off. Like Dorothy and Toto, who found a new life on the Yellow Brick Road. He would put on Grampa's old helmet, daydream, and say things like, "Rapunzel, Rapunzel, let down your hair." Or he'd sing along to Grampa's old tunes. ♪Get your motor runnin'◇.

"Incredible things are happening in the world," Grampa told the boy. "I saw many of them riding that motorcycle."

* * *

Following high school graduation, Trent left home in the back seat of Dad's grey Toyota Corolla. Mr. Weber said, "We got you this far, son. Now it's up to you."

Manfred didn't plead; he didn't have a voice, more of a squeak. Often, he just pointed and gestured. Grampa said, "Don't worry. Lean into the wind and things work out."

The parents deposited their only child three hundred miles from home in a cheap room, the rent prepaid for one term. Except for Grampa, Trent left behind no memories of affection. He imagined Northwest Technical College as his Yellow Brick Road.

As suggested by Grampa, the boy registered in Auto Mechanics. He could picture himself as a monkey wrencher, although he was disheveled, even for a grease monkey, poorly nourished, homely as hell, and awkward. But what Trent had acquired was a thick skin. He wore a skullcap and quickly found the shop more to his liking than the high school cafeteria.

"Then he fell in love," Patty told me. "With nuts and bolts. A Yamaha scooter."

Grampa had presented his eighteen-year-old grandson with a used Zuma. Also, an extra-large white flip-up helmet. "I'll roll my old Harley out of the garage and we'll ride, one of these days." He never did, because "it needs too much work." Still, Grampa was a lifesaver—he threw his grandson motorcycles.

On melancholy days, Trent no longer nursed despair; he had an escape—climb on. Give expectations the finger. He is of average height with a slim build. With his head covered, the young man had an agreeable presence. "A grandparent present," he said about his flip-up. "Planning to get a Vega Vintage."

Trent joined an online scooter forum, and a community welcomed him.

Coordination; how often we curse the gods for not getting enough of it. But on two wheels, Trent had perfect balance. Lopsided no more! Scooter Boy stood, raised his legs, pointed his arms, hopped about, and did wheelies. Soon he was giving Northwest Technical College lot regulations the biker salute. Students embraced their outlaw.

Sometimes Trent took his helmet off and waved. He wore a black bandanna "to keep stuff out."

When Patty finished the story, I thought, Ugly duckling to scooter swan. Thanks to a small motorcycle, he discovered his raison d'être.

Transformations can begin with a tarp pulled back. An engine that hasn't run in years. A boy with one ear too many climbing aboard something bigger than himself. Maybe that's all it takes: two wheels and the audacity to imagine going forward.

Motorcycles can't fix you, but they can point the way. They say: here's a path. Twist the throttle. See where it goes.

My Motorcycle State of Mind: Saved by cycle.

* * *

"Trent works at Southside Motorcycles now," Patty had told me. "The owner took him under his wing."

"Customers want a confident voice," his boss instructed, and the Southside Scooter Kid stopped whispering.

Patty showed me a pic of the young man clad in his sponsor's gear. "Has his own YouTube channel, Southside Scooter." Patty played an episode. "A voice! A voice! It's his tagline. Let the wheels speak."

"He's a showman and a teacher."

"Motorcycles saved him. Makes me cherish mine even more. Wonder how he would have ended up if not for Grampa and the Shovelhead," Patty's friend said.

He'd be locked in a dingy tower. A Jack without magical beans. Or like Mark, rooted beside the World's Largest Spruce Tree.

Patty and her friends rode south toward Eugene. Our fortuitous encounter had me thinking about how it's possible to be saved by cycle. How one shouldn't shuffle along with platitudes.

I showed Cam and Tony a Scooter Boy YouTube video.

"Bet I could do that," Cam said.

"You're on," Tony said. "A Tart of the Month every month for a year or you clean the grill."

They appointed me the judge.

"If you tilt your head this way, it looks more like a motorcycle." I was showing Conrad my crustacean art. I displayed it on a shelf below *Motorcycle on Velvet*.

"Cheesy Mexican, you say? Sounds like a worthwhile ride."

"May as well go further and add a slice of honest pie."

Conrad studied the calendar on his phone. "Can you get away the week of the twelfth?"

"Cam's attempting his stunt on the fourteenth."

We agreed on the seventeenth.

30

Immunity

I'm not good at assimilation. I don't identify with causes, movements, or organizations in an intimate way. I'm at ease with mutts and the legion of bikers, but at times, I find even them intolerable.

Motorcycle interactions can be grating. Jabber is jabber, whether about politics, sports, work, or bikes. Gibberish causes me to mutter. ***Find someone who cares and tell them. Just not me.***

Marta cares. She is immune to jabber.

Perceptions, popular culture, and a yearning to be heard shape much of what people say, not experience or research.

This is why I love my motorcycles. Fire up the engine. Ride off. No jabbering. Until you stop, but by then, you've built up immunity.

I've heard Marta say, "Riding is when I finally hear silence." She doesn't mean the absence of noise—it's the absence of demands. No expectations, no replies needed, no jabber bouncing back at you. Just the rumble, the road, and being with the version of yourself that makes sense. Motorcycles can re-tune your world.

They make the world do what my mother called "cease and desist." Conversations often produce stress. On-motorcycle, you ride alone. Your relationship with the world is altered. You can tune your state of mind one thought, each perception, one turn at a time.

Marta maintains an air of credibility when she speaks that often makes me feel I have loose lips. Off-motorcycle you must speak substantive words or keep quiet! I say things that are extraordinarily dumb. I emit gibberish. Motorcycles solve that problem.

As I readied for coffee with Marta at Tony's, my state of mind was *insecure jabber*.

I was naked. Stake-less. These things happen out of the blue, Marta, and nothing happened. Yes, I was receptive, but nothing. I will remain one of those without purpose. I don't care. Really Marta, I don't care!

As we mature, we have intentions that are like bowling pins: make money, have sex, find a home to have sex and get wasted in, and so on. Over time, the pins of life are cleared or become less compelling. Relaxation time arrives. No need to be constantly driven. Chill out a bit. Give mindfulness a go—until you realize wind therapy is far more effective.

All is well, but then a Marta urges you to tune yourself up and adopt a reason for being. Keep yourself from rusting away. Do not park in the Complacency Towers lot, The Home of People Without a Raison d'Être. Keep your tank well fueled!

What about me? Maybe I'm not lost—just uninterested in being found. Don't need an answer—just need a reason to ride.

I remember a group of Christians bikers once invited me to join their prayer circle. In a motel parking lot, they blessed my ride. It was uplifting, and their religious fellowship was invigorating. It happened out of the blue, an opportunity for me to latch onto something solid. But I remained unconvinced. I'd have to join their club, and organized groups always get my goat with their regulations and formalities.

Perhaps I'm a misfit? An Oddball? Or perhaps I must look closer to the ground. Find something without rules or rituals.

As I looked at my **crustacean** art display, it hit me. The idea spun around in my head. I will carry on doing motorcycle stuff. Life is a journey. Ride! It's not complicated, Marta. Motion is enough.

* * *

"Ride!" In the garage, I shouted the word to Pearl and Bunny with great enthusiasm. Then I did the playful shifting movement that Pearl likes. "Ride, Pearl. Keep riding!" Bunny, being a cat, remained unimpressed. Dogs, not so much.

I'd had my raison d'être all along—stick to your knitting, what you know and love. I'm a better person when I ride.

"Ride," I repeated. Life should be a beautiful way of dying. What could be better than riding it out?

I picked up Bunny and sat beside Neuro. "It won't be constant, Bunny. I must pace myself and enjoy other things. But there will be boots on my feet and no room for regrets in my top box (once I fix the locking mechanism). When death calls, it'll have to chase me down the road."

Bunny's expression said, *That's nice, but I really don't care.* Pearl celebrated my enthusiasm.

"Instead of aging out, I'll push back. Body and soul."

Or not.

Stakes in the ground are often not realized; it's about the pursuit.

My Motorcycle State of Mind: Immortal!

"You see, Marta," I said, practicing with Bunny and Pearl, "my revolvement isn't complicated." I'm already doing it. Just carry on."

There would be snickers from the gang at Tony's. *That's all he's got?* C'est la vie.

When you have a raison d'être, you are resilient.

I'd wear my tee shirt. The one that says: **I Don't Care.**

31

So What?

"So," Marta asked. "How was it? You look relaxed." My ride glow was fading, but a smirk remained. "Like someone at ease. You've moved on?"

Ancient history, Marta. The only direction is forward. I nodded yes.

A wondrous aroma filled Tony's Bistro. My roll arrived, fresh from the oven. "Thanks, Elena. Been looking forward to this. Brought you a little something." I unwrapped a crab shell. "Crustacean art featuring a cake." Elena's expression conveyed "extremely impressive."

"Thank you so much, Michael."

It's true. Home is where your friends are—and where the world's best rolls come fresh from the oven.

Marta had a pastel de nata.

"I have a shell with a motorcycle for you. It's in my garage."

"Good trip?" Den arrived and greeted me as if I'd returned from touring the Stans.

I nodded, tore off a hunk of doughy bun, and pointed—magnificent. Into my mouth it went. For a moment, the universe and I embraced.

My Motorcycle State of Mind? Grateful.

After swallowing, I said, "Over the moon, you could say. That's me. In Astoria, I met a local who told me about an ancient Camino pilgrimage route in Europe called the Spiritual Variant. 'For me it was far more than the sum of the pathways, people, religion, weather, and all,' she said. That's how I feel about my trip. Somehow, it was more than road miles. Road trips change you in ways that can't be plotted. The miles don't just pass under your tires—they pass through you. You return in the same gear, on the same bike, but with something changed. Maybe lighter or heavier and not noticed until you've put the kickstand down. After a sip of coffee, I added, "What's up with you guys?" Tony pulled up a chair.

Marta winked.

"Gotta go," Tony announced. "We have a trip planned ... to Alaska."

"Guzzi's going to Alaska?"

"Join us? Den's thinking about coming."

Den nodded.

Marta can be like Mother Goose or the Old Lady Who Lived in a Shoe, who kissed her children and sent them to bed. She's always warm and inclusive. Come into the shoe. Commune. Rest on my soul.

"Thanks for asking, but no. There's a lot of wildlife up there. I've moved on, but Alaska would be like sending an alcoholic to a bar." Also mosquitoes. "Bull of the Woods country."

Conrad and Earl arrived and asked Elena, "Any buns left?"

Elena nodded and showed her present. "I'd guess it's a shortened cake."

I was pleased. The shell guaranteed my place in the gooey bun queue.

"Pound cake?" Conrad guessed.

When Marta and I were alone, Marta said, "It's great ... you're standing tall, on the pegs again."

"On the trip, I realized, I've become a different rider—since the accident. But one who enjoys riding just as much ... maybe more. As you'd say, my disposition has evolved." It's complicated, like trying to understand the essence of quality. I fidgeted with my yin-yang keychain and looked at Marta's Cheshire Cat smile. "Balancing the three A's." Awareness, Appreciation, and Adrenalin. Then silence. I imagined we were sharing the same thought: The wheels are round and they roll. No jabber needed.

32

The Final Revolvement

May your ride be joyful and your Motorcycle State of Mind be both at ease and spirited.

Perhaps we'll meet on the road. Or share a slice of honest pie?

Gotta Go?

Don't let the itch pass.

ADDENDIX: Break In Procedure

The procedures below are recommended when breaking in your new book. Follow all interval and general instructions for optimal engagement.

GENERAL INSTRUCTIONS

Use the motorcycle salute and other expressive gestures to offset any sections you find unpleasant.

Read each paragraph with an open mind and your helmet off. If you hit a rough patch, do not slam on the brakes. Maintain posture, and keep your eyes on the lines ahead.

Occasionally lean into a series of page turns and speed-read your way out.

If you experience the Ass Problem, switch to a standing reading position.

INTERVALS

FOR THE FIRST 50 PAGES or 12,500 WORDS: Avoid exceeding three-quarters reading capacity. Vary your reading pace often. Refrain from aggressive page flips. Cruise, avoiding hill climbs and drag races.

AT PAGE 100 or 25,000 WORDS: Begin reading at full comprehension for short bursts. Change your dictionary. Upgrade to one with fresh lemmatization and premium collocations.

You may now safely read this book in public.
END OF BOOK

The book will end—you can't change it. But the ride is yours.

Books By The Author

Scraping Pegs, The Truth About Motorcycles

The Joy of Motorcycles, More Scraping Pegs

Scrape Your Lists, The Motorcycle Files

Motorcycle State of Mind, Beyond Scraping Pegs

The Motorcycle Prescription, Scrape Your Therapy

Book Information: Scraping Pegs on Facebook

www.ingramcontent.com/pod-product-compliance
Lightning Source LLC
Chambersburg PA
CBHW071344080526
44587CB00017B/2962